Endorsements

"Churches, ministries, and artists with a passion to reach lost souls should, before they do anything else, consult this book. It will help define and shape your ministry and evangelism strategy."

—*Rory Noland, author of* Heart of the Artist

"Most people know God is creative. But many Christians don't realize that evangelism should reflect God's creativity. It is so often missing. Modern culture often communicates through art forms. How can we not see art as central to our outreach efforts? That is why I am so thankful that Con wrote this book. He joins the arts and the mission of God together—as they should be. Artists don't have to feel alone any longer, but can feel like a valuable part of a larger church community and the mission of Jesus. *Outreach and the Artist* is a beautiful palette of theology, mission, and creative arts mixed together. May many artists not only read this book, but may many lives be changed as a result of those who put into practice what is within its pages."

—*Dan Kimball, author of* They Like Jesus but Not the Church *and* Adventures in Churchland

"What does Jazz have to do with Jesus and what does Picasso have to do with Paul? If anyone knows, it is Con Campbell since he uniquely traverses the diverse worlds of artists, churches, and the academy. Campbell shows how the gospel can come with, to, and through the arts. While artists constitute a peculiar subculture of their own, Campbell explains how the gospel can resonate with artists of all types, and how the gospel can reverberate through the craft of painters, drummers, and actors for the glory of God. Anyone who is involved in inner-city ministry, who wants to explore creative forms of outreach, or just wants to know how to connect churches with artists is going to want to read this book."

—*Dr. Michael F. Bird, Lecturer in Theology at Ridley Melbourne Ministry & Mission College, Australia*

"I first heard this material in talks Con gave on the subject, and I am thrilled to know his wisdom on reaching out through (and to) the arts will gain a wider audience. Con is an artist's artist and a scholar's scholar—a rare combination and a pure gift to the body of Christ."

—*John Dickson, author of* Humilitas

OUTREACH AND THE ARTIST

CON CAMPBELL

OUTREACH AND THE ARTIST

SHARING THE GOSPEL WITH THE ARTS

ZONDERVAN.com/
AUTHORTRACKER
follow your favorite authors

ZONDERVAN

Outreach and the Artist

This title is also available as a Zondervan ebook. Visit www.zondervan.com/ebooks.

Requests for information should be addressed to:

Zondervan, *Grand Rapids, Michigan 49530*

Library of Congress Cataloging-in-Publication Data

Campbell, Constantine R.
Outreach and the artist : sharing the gospel with the arts / Constantine R. Campbell.
pages cm
ISBN 978-0-310-49496-6 (softcover)
1. Jazz—Religious aspects. 2. Christianity and the arts. I. Title.
ML3921.8.J39C36 2013
261.5'7—dc23 2012042780

Any Internet addresses (websites, blogs, etc.) and telephone numbers in this book are offered as a resource. They are not intended in any way to be or imply an endorsement by Zondervan, nor does Zondervan vouch for the content of these sites and numbers for the life of this book.

Cover design: Micah Kandros Design
Cover photography: iStockphoto
Interior design: Matthew Van Zomeren

Printed in the United States of America

---

13 14 15 16 17 18 19 /DCI/ 20 19 18 17 16 15 14 13 12 11 10 9 8 7 6 5 4 3 2 1

For David McDonald

CONTENTS

INTRODUCTION

The arts are a precious gift of God. Music, painting, dance, sculpture, theater, and so many other art forms enrich our lives and give expression to the human condition. They challenge and comfort us. They inspire and humble us. They feed us and demand our energies. I can't imagine life without the arts. What a miserable and shallow existence that would be!

I listen to music whenever I can: working at my desk, driving the car, or walking down the street. I'm listening to Pat Metheny and Chris Potter right now as I write this introduction. If I don't get a decent shot of jazz each day, it affects my mood and mental health. And I'm confident that many reading this book will relate to that to some extent, if not quite as obsessively.

As a Christian I am thankful to God for many things, not just the arts. Even more significant than the life-enriching arts is the life-resurrecting work of Jesus Christ. Nothing is more precious than the gift of forgiveness, relationship with God, eternal life, membership in the body of Christ, and the privilege to serve the true and living God. Part of our service to God involves our outreach to those who do not yet know Jesus Christ as Lord and Savior. If you're reading this book, I assume that you too are interested in—perhaps deeply committed to—reaching out to friends, family, and wider communities with the good news of Jesus.

The arts and outreach. In this book, I want to bring those two things together. Many Christian artists have employed their gifts and abilities for the task of outreach, but there has been comparatively little written about it. By writing this book, I hope to encourage artists to make use of their gifts for evangelism and help them to think through the issues involved in doing that. I also want to encourage pastors and "ordinary" church folk to engage with the arts and the artistic people in their midst for the sake of outreach.

There are three main concerns in the book: evangelism *with*, *through*, and *to* the arts.

Evangelism with the Arts

Chapters 2 and 3 relate to evangelism *with* the arts. Christian artists are often untapped resources for evangelistic endeavor. While their abilities may be utilized in service of the church in various ways (e.g., congregational worship), it is not always obvious to churches that artists have enormous potential for outreach. First, artists can use their abilities for the proclamation of the gospel to music lovers and art aficionados, or to the general public who are happy to attend a church-sponsored cultural event, such as a jazz night or gallery opening. Second, artists have access to otherwise closed artistic subcultures. They can become missionaries to their own people in a way that nonartists cannot.

Evangelism through the Arts

Chapter 4 relates to evangelism *through* the arts. Artistic ability can be a powerful tool for the proclamation of the gospel, and artistic mediums have enormous potential for fresh approaches to outreach. Because the arts tap into the human condition in profound ways, they represent a unique avenue through which to address the big questions of life. Furthermore, people's natural love for the arts provides a connection point to the unbeliever that is nonthreatening, engaging of heart and mind, and sometimes deeply personal.

Evangelism to the Arts

Chapters 5, 6, and 7 relate to evangelism *to* the arts. Artistic networks form tightly knit subcultures in our society that are sometimes impenetrable to outsiders. As such, they can resemble "unreached people-groups" in that these subcultures often have no Christian witness or presence and tend to be shut off from conventional methods of outreach. Evangelism *to* the arts is for the purpose of reaching these unreached subcultures.

My Limitations

To understand further what this book is about, it is worth explaining how I have come to the point of writing it. More than anything else I've dared to put in print to date, this book is quite autobiographical. In some places it just sounds like me talking about me (to which my friends will say, "What's new?"). And I want to apologize about that up front.

But at the same time, this book exists only because of

the fairly odd set of circumstances that God has put me in during the course of my life and the experiences he has used to teach me about evangelism, artists, and bringing the two together. I'm really no expert on evangelism, and I'm not particularly an expert on the arts either. But on the relationship between the two, I think I have something to say that hasn't yet been said – since so little has been said on the topic.

My experience with the arts and evangelism over the years gives me license to pontificate on the subject for the rest of this book. The book consists of a collection of principles that I believe are generally true about the arts and outreach, illustrated mostly by personal anecdotes. While there are obvious limitations involved in using one's own anecdotes, these are the stories, incidents, and experiences that have caused me to reflect on the issue at hand. They are the reason I'm able to write this at all, so they're worth sharing. One of the limitations of my own experience is that it is related to music, and jazz in particular. But that ought not diminish the value of the insights gained about the arts in general. Please "translate" my jazz experiences to reflect on other forms of artistic endeavor, whatever you happen to be interested in. This is *not* a book about jazz, though you might get that impression as you read on.

Artist Profiles

My limitations and personal anecdotes are offset by a collection of artist profiles. A wonderfully diverse and gifted group of Christian artists have contributed their thoughts to this project in a personal and reflective manner. The profiles are interviews, based around a set of questions. Each artist has responded to these questions in their own way, using their own words. They offer reflections derived from a wide variety of artistic endeavors, and they share some of the experience, wisdom, and inspiration that have marked their lives as Christians in the arts.

Theology

The final thing to add here is that the discussion of outreach and the arts is grounded in an understanding of the Bible. While I don't intend to present a theological treatise in what follows, there is a lot of theology at work in the background. In fact, there are two specific spheres of theological thought that impact this topic.

The first is the doctrine of creation. I believe that the arts are part of God's good creation. They are to be respected, appreciated, cherished, and used for the good of humanity to the glory of God. There will be no arts bashing in this book, because a theological understanding of the arts won't allow it. Having said that, there is a dark side to the arts because we live in a fallen world. In the hands of rebellious people, whose hearts are set against God, even his good and wonderful gifts can become powerful instruments for evil. This is sadly true of the arts in many ways, but we must not therefore condemn the arts themselves. They remain a good, ordered part of creation; if they are abused and distorted for imperfect purposes, this is due to maltreatment that is not intrinsic to their nature.

Second, the Bible shapes our understanding of evangelism. Evangelism is the proclamation of the life, death, resurrection, and ascension of Jesus Christ the Lord. He died for our sins and rose again to give us new life. He will return to judge the living and the dead. When I refer to evangelism in this book, this is the message I have in mind. While there's an important place for apologetics and for speaking about various other biblical truths as we engage with unbelievers, evangelism is the proclamation of the *evangel*—the good news, the gospel. From here on, this definition of outreach is assumed.

Furthermore, the Bible's teaching of God's sovereignty and work of predestination in salvation gird an understanding of evangelism. I realize there are differing viewpoints about predestination. Nevertheless, I wish to be clear that for all the talk about how to do evangelism with, through, and to the arts, I am operating under the conviction that God alone can save. His Spirit works in those he has chosen, and through the proclamation of the gospel, the elect are brought to saving faith in Christ.

While the book is practical—in the sense of discussing our strategies, understanding of artists, and going forward in outreach—this does not mean that it is ultimately up to us to see people saved. God is sovereign, and he will bring about his purposes. Our job is to be faithful and fulfill the works of service he has chosen to give us. In his grace, believers are mercifully included in a partnership with God for the task of growing his church. He does not rely on us, but we are involved nonetheless.*

---

* For further reflection on the theme of our involvement in the work of God in evangelism, see the classic book of J. I. Packer, *Evangelism and the Sovereignty of God* (Downers Grove, IL: InterVarsity Press, 2010).

I pray this book will encourage, edify, and inspire you in your engagement with the arts and outreach. It's certainly not the last word on the topic, but I hope it is a helpful first word.

CHAPTER 1

A JAZZ TESTIMONIAL

I was an artist before I was a Christian. My artistic life began at age ten, when I became obsessed with drawing cartoons, inspired by reading and loving Garfield cartoons by Jim Davis. I developed my own comic strip, complete with characters, plots, bad jokes, and the rest. By age twelve I had drawn over two hundred cartoons in my series. Before I turned twelve, the series had been considered seriously for publication in a local newspaper, but was knocked back because of my age.

Around that time I started to get serious about painting and had a private art tutor who taught me how to handle oils, pencils, and watercolors. I worked on still lifes and a few portraits. By this time, art was more important than school or anything else. At age twelve I moved to a different city with my family, and some of my cartoons were published in a local newspaper. Shortly after that I lost interest in the visual arts—for the time being, anyway. I got into athletics and at age fifteen competed in the state championships for the 800 meters.

But something else had been bubbling beneath the surface from age twelve. I had started to learn the saxophone. I had learned piano from age six, but wasn't really into it. The saxophone was different. It was fun and I practiced regularly. By age fifteen I had gotten pretty good at it. Then I discovered jazz. One of my uncles gave me a Stan Getz record and I listened to it, and only it, for a full year. By age sixteen I had become hooked on jazz, was learning to improvise, and was practicing hard. Before long I had decided to become a professional jazz musician once school was finished. In my final two years at school, I was practicing between four and six hours a day. I barely bothered with schoolwork and couldn't wait for it to be over so I could go to jazz school. I had also rediscovered the visual arts, working on a sculpture for my high school certificate on a major work consisting of some old instruments that I pulled apart and welded into a big treble clef.

For many musicians, music begins in the church. For me it was reverse. Music led me to church. In my second-to-last year at school, a hip, young music teacher came to teach at my school. Miss Benn breathed new life into our school's music department with positivity and enthusiasm. I had a mild crush on her, like most of the other guys. Anyway, because I was good at saxophone, she asked me to do a few gigs with her band. Turns out it was a Christian band. The guys in the band were great people—fine musicians, but really on about Jesus. Eventually they took me with them to their church, and throughout my last year of school I was going to church each Sunday night. I thought I was a Christian, but the truth was that I had little to no understanding of Christian faith—not helped by the fact that the church did not really teach the Bible. My true god was Jazz, and I didn't see any problem with that.

When I finished school, I moved to Canberra to study Jazz Performance at the Canberra School of Music of the Australian National University. I had been going to church the year before this, so I figured I would find a church in Canberra. I picked one at random out of the phone book and went along. From my point of view, it couldn't have been more random, but now I see God's hand in it. For the first time in my life, I heard the Bible taught clearly, and it blew me away. While I was progressing in my jazz studies and being confirmed in my idolatry (more on this later), simultaneously something else was bubbling beneath the surface. I was becoming a Christian.

By the end of my first year of studies at jazz school, I had become a Christian, had starting dating my future wife, Bronwyn, and was wrestling with the place of jazz in my life. It was becoming increasingly clear that jazz had been occupying the place of a god in my life, and as a fast-growing Christian this would not do. And so the battle between Jazz and Jesus was underway. I wanted to be a Christian and wasn't going to give up on Jesus, but I had become used to my life revolving around music. The more I studied the Bible and was involved in church, the more unsettled I became. I fluctuated between thinking that I had to give up jazz altogether and thinking that God wanted me to be a professional jazz musician for his glory.

In my second year of studies, I won the prestigious James Morrison Jazz Scholarship, which is awarded each year to one jazz musician in Australia (of any instrument) at age nineteen. To win that competition had been my goal since I was sixteen, and I took it as a sign that God wanted me to be a jazz musician after all. Why would he allow me to win if that *wasn't* the plan?

It wasn't the plan. In my third year of university the question came up again in a big way. I went to a midyear Bible conference for university students, called The Focal Point. My pastor, Dave McDonald, taught the Bible that week on the theme of the church. It was seriously good Bible teaching, and I was deeply challenged from the first day. The challenge was that believers should not be building their own Tower of Babel, but be concerned for the building of God's church. Working as copartners with God in the building of his church is actually the first vocation of all Christians.

I knew that I had been building my own little Tower of Babel in the form of my jazz career. It was my own little kingdom, and while I wanted it to be for God's glory, deep down I suspected it was for my own. During the next few days I prayed a lot, talked a lot, and determined to sort out my priorities once and for all. On the last day of the conference, Dave challenged us again. He argued that if, as had been established, we should be focused on serving the church, the next question is how best to do that. For some people, it would mean being a solid Christian in the workplace. For others it would mean doing so as a student. For others, it might mean changing your job. For some it would mean quitting their careers and going into full-time Christian ministry.

Well, my number was up. I knew that I could better serve the church in full-time ministry than as a full-time musician. Sure, there would have been lots of ministry to do as a musician, and I know Christian musicians who do that well. But for *me*, there wasn't any question: my heart was changed, and I wanted to go into full-time ministry.

After The Focal Point, I talked to Dave about my new desire to go into ministry, and he told me to come back in a month. If I still felt this way, then we'd talk. A month later, we talked and decided that the following year I would begin work with him as a ministry apprentice. Two weeks after my jazz studies concluded, Bron and I got married, and after the summer I began working in full-time Christian ministry. The jazz god had been put down; Jesus won that contest, and life would continue without music. Or so I thought.

It turns out that God had other plans. He used my abilities in music for ministry in ways that I could not have predicted. I kept playing lots of "secular" gigs while doing ministry work full-time, but the big surprise was the way that jazz would become a powerful tool for evangelism. The way all that happened comes later, but for now I will say that God blessed me with the combination of two great loves: playing jazz and talking to people about Jesus. I didn't dream it was possible, and in fact I initially thought it was a crazy idea. But God has given me many opportunities to serve him with (and without) a saxophone in my hands. For that I am very grateful. As Fiona McDonald (Dave's wife) once said to me: "You gave up jazz for God, and he gave it right back to you." So true. But when God gave it back to me, it was with a higher purpose than it had ever had before.

Alissa Noelle Photography

Artist Profile: Keeley Manca Lambert

www.keeleymancalambert.com

1. **Describe your artistic interests.**
   Acting—more specifically, comedy, improv, and realism. I have a Bachelor of Fine Arts in Acting from Texas State University. I have also been singing and dancing my whole life. I dabble in songwriting, along with singing and playing the guitar.

2. **What struggles have you had as a Christian engaged with the arts?**
   There are quite a few struggles I've had as a Christ-follower engaged in the arts. For example, I don't feel completely understood by the acting culture or

the Christian culture. When it comes to the acting world, I haven't completely surrendered my life to the lifestyle that most actors have. There are certain lines I'm not willing to cross, there are sacrifices I am not willing to make, and my whole life isn't wrapped up in "making it big."

In the Christian world, there are few who understand what it looks like to actually be a part of the artistic culture, or "worldly culture." I think a lot of Christians are confused, or maybe just inexperienced, when it comes to dealing with actors, and I'm some type of weird hybrid ... a Christ-following actor, but not involved in Christian Film/Theater.

When do I speak in truth and when do I speak in love? I think a lot of Christians encounter this problem; it's not necessarily specific to the arts.

A key passage for my life is 1 Corinthians 9:22–23: "I have become all things to all people, that by all means I might save some. I do it all for the sake of the gospel, that I may share in its blessings." A big challenge that I've come across while in the arts is discerning which parts of the actor's lifestyle I take on and which parts I separate myself from. I have a desire to be good at what I do and to reach actors at their level. I don't want to be someone who is "above," looking down on them because I'm a Christian. I want them to see me as their peer, as someone they can trust. On the flip side, I want to be sensitive to the Spirit when it comes to making decisions about things I do with my friends or what roles I decide to take on.

I am a firm believer that actors have been given the role of storytellers and mirrors of the human story. The human story is not always pretty and nice. In order to see goodness, truth, and redemption, we must see evil and the disparity of human nature, and sometimes those are the roles I take on. I always try to tread carefully and ask for wisdom from the Holy Spirit concerning which of those roles I should accept.

3. Describe the ministry you've been able to have through the arts.

I've been acting since I was ten years old. I grew up attending a Christian school, and I lived in a Christian bubble, fearful to venture outside of that culture. I thought unbelievers were aliens who spoke a different language and had a different lifestyle, and I had no interest in trying to relate to them. When I graduated from high school, I had never had a single non-Christian friend.

I started my freshman year of college at one of the biggest party schools in Texas. I knew that the Lord had called me to minister in the Theater, but I had no idea how to do that. I would attend my acting classes and get out of there as soon as possible. In my sophomore year I was cast as a lead in one of our main stage productions, so I was thrown into this world of actors. I began to ask the Lord how to reach these people who were so foreign and unknown to me, but whom He wanted me to serve. For the next three years I began to intentionally love and serve the people in Theater, not viewing them as my little "conversion projects," but as real people with real hurts. These actors soon became my family whom I loved deeply.

After college the Lord made a way for me to move to New York City to be a part of a new faith-based nonprofit group in the arts, Transform. Transform is a community of artists, from young emerging to established artists, seeking to wrestle with the deep questions of art, faith, and culture. I am pursuing professional acting with intentionality and for the sake of the gospel.

The biggest ministry I have had in the arts through all of these years has been the art of listening. People are tired of being talked at. Christians have been talking at people for a long time, and now it's time to listen. Dr. Henry Cloud says, "To empathize and validate what someone is experiencing does not mean that you always agree or even think that the other person is right. It just means that you see it as *valid in that it is really their experience*, and true for that person, and you show them that you understand what they are thinking and feeling."* People want someone who will listen to them and fight for

---

* Henry Cloud, *Integrity* (New York: Collins, 2006), 64.

them. I've found that the Holy Spirit has moved the most when I've shut my mouth and listened.

4. Concerning other artists you know, what is the single biggest barrier stopping them from coming to Christ?

The single biggest barrier stopping artists from coming to Christ is Christians. The artist community has a large population of homosexuals, and of course artists are going to stand up for those they love, because they see them as family. One of the main things artists think when they think of the Christian community is homosexual hatred. Now, I am not condoning homosexuality, but I do think that we have to stop trying to "fix" someone or their sexuality before they can come to Christ. Jesus doesn't go after our actions. He wants our hearts first, and the Holy Spirit will then help to transform the heart into outward actions.

Many artists have also been hurt by the church or by Christians whom they have come across in their own lives. They see hypocrisy on television, in politics, and in their local community. Christians are not perfect by any means, but we have got to look at our own hearts before we look at the actions of others. It is the power of the Holy Spirit that is going to change the lives of the lost, not our expectations of how they should live.

CHAPTER 2

OUTREACH *WITH* THE ARTS

What does jazz have to do with Jesus?

This was the question I pondered when I was first asked to put together an evangelistic jazz night. It was the year 2000, and I was in my second year of study at Moore Theological College, Sydney. Each year, Moore sends out mission teams to various churches around Sydney and beyond, and my mission team was heading to the Anglican Church in South Coogee, on Sydney's coastline. The minister of that church, Geoff Deutscher, met with the mission team a few weeks beforehand so that we could get to know him and make some plans for the mission. He had heard that there was a jazz musician on the team.

He asked, "So, I've heard there's a great jazz musician on the team – who would that be?"

I sheepishly put up my hand and mumbled something like: "I don't know if I'm *great*."

He immediately said, "I have an idea for a fantastic mission outreach event: a jazz night! We'll advertise it throughout Coogee and make it the big event of the mission. It'll be great! Everyone will come; people love jazz! I'd like you to put a concert together and during the show you could do some talking about Jesus."

I thought he was crazy. The problem seemed obvious: *What does jazz have to do with Jesus?* How would I possibly "do jazz" and then just start talking about Jesus? Nuts.

I said to Geoff, "I don't know about this. How would I go from playing jazz to talking about Jesus? I don't see it."

"I'm sure you'll work something out," he said. "Maybe you could talk about what's great about jazz, but then say why Jesus is even greater!"

I thought that was a dumb idea. But at least he was enthusiastic. In the end, of course, I had no choice and the "jazz night" was born.

Two hundred and fifty jazz nights later, I realize that Geoff Deutscher saw something that I – the artist – could not see for myself at the time: there is huge potential to marry the arts with the message of Jesus. After that first concert at his church, I understood it for myself, and I haven't looked back.

In this chapter I want to encourage pastors and church folk to think about the artists in your midst and how you can partner with them in the missional calling of the church. I also want to address the artist side of that partnership, since it takes two to tango. The partnership between a church and an artist/artists is not as straightforward as it sounds, and there are issues to navigate from both sides. This will be true regardless of whether the artist/artists are "homegrown" in one's own church or are invited from outside.

Harnessing the Outreach Potential of the Artist

If you think there is homegrown talent in your church and you want to encourage them to engage in outreach, you may need to do some groundwork first. Like me, some artists might need to be persuaded that their art form can be used for evangelism. In fact, as far as I can tell, there are few high-caliber Christian artists who have thoughtfully reflected on how to use their gifts for the purpose of outreach. Don't get me wrong; there are plenty of Christian artists who want to use their gifts to serve the Lord and the church. But this will often be conducted as ministry for *Christians*.

Lots of singer-songwriters, for example, can imagine themselves hitting the road on the Christian music circuit, playing their Christian songs for churches, youth groups, and Christian events. Christian actors and playwrights might likewise take their Christian dramas and skits on the church circuit, and so on. Of course this is a great thing, and it's a wonderful way for believers to use their gifts for the edification of the church. But that's not what I'm talking about. I'm talking about *outreach*.

The problem I had with the idea of using jazz for outreach was *seeing the connection* between the two things. I had trouble conceiving how it would work. That will almost certainly be a problem for an artist who may be willing but reluctant: *How will it work?* I have encountered this issue a number of times over the years. As I've worked up new concerts with new talks, it is the perennial problem to be solved. And I've seen others struggle with it.

Recently, a friend emailed me for help with this exact issue. He is a jazz drummer living in New York. His church had decided to host an evangelistic jazz concert and asked him to put something together. He identified "the problem" right away and asked for advice. How could he give a talk that would move from jazz to Jesus? I mentioned a few angles I've used before and gave him permission to copy freely.

Sadly, others have copied without asking. I was once invited by a local church to bring a band and do my thing for a jazz night they were planning. In discussions with the church, they asked what my angle would be. When I told them about *Freedom in the Groove*, they said that someone had used that exact same theme at their church the year before. I had been copied! I don't mind, but my point is that it's difficult to come up with a good angle, which is why some copycats out there have used my material; they couldn't think of an angle of their own. Imitation is the highest form of flattery, I guess.

Artists can be precious souls, so it may be better not to hold a gun to their head and say: "You're doing it – work it out!" But if you can cast a vision of what might be possible, with enough time and space their creative juices will take care of the rest. The point is, it *can* be done, and an artist first of all needs to know that it's possible. There may be examples you can point to, or you could give them this book to read. It doesn't matter. What matters is that artists have successfully done this kind of thing before, and you want your artist to develop a great, unique, and special way to use their gifts for outreach. My guess is that once an artist sees or hears of such an event, he or she will start to critique it and decide how they would have done it better. Once that happens, they're on their way. But more on this later.

Your artist may also need some persuading about how appealing their craft is to the general public. When Geoff Deutscher said to me, "Everyone will come; people love jazz!" I thought, "No, people hate jazz. No one will come." And to an extent, I was right. Even in America – sadly – jazz lovers form a small contingent of sane society. At big jazz concerts, audiences typically consist of a high number of jazz musicians – at least half of most jazz audiences are other jazz musicians.* This has often caused me to wonder whether jazz is just music for musicians, since no one else really seems to be interested. But that's a topic for another day. My point is that a second potential problem in recruiting an artist for outreach is that they may feel that their art form is a bit obscurantist, poorly understood, esoteric, and definitely not mainstream. The more "artistic" the artist, the more this will be true.

But Geoff was right that people will love jazz and will come, and herein lies the beauty of it all. With some clever marketing, the most obscure, misunderstood, and unpopular art form – like jazz! – can be a hit in any community. Its obscurity can become its selling point. How often do people get to see live jazz – let alone in their own neighborhood? Not only that, but the artist is going to explain what it's all about and how it all works. You'd never get that at a "real" jazz concert! Someone will say, "Oh, I've always wanted to understand what jazz is about!" The fact is, a high number of churches I've visited have reported that our jazz night was

---

* This statistic is completely made up.

the most "successful" outreach event of the year. They had more guests from outside the church than any other event. In fact, it is not unusual for the proportion of guests at such jazz nights to be over fifty percent of the audience.* Other outreach events struggle to achieve such numbers.

There Is *Always* an Angle

In my view, there will always be a way to connect the arts to outreach. No matter how obscure the art form — whether it uses words or lyrics, and regardless of whether it is aural or visual — it is possible to find a connection between the arts and the gospel. How can I make such a bold claim? It's simple, really. The arts are about life. And because the arts are about life, they relate to Jesus, because Jesus is about life.

What do I mean, "The arts are about life"? There are some art forms — I can imagine someone saying — that seem to have no meaning whatsoever. Even the artist doesn't know what it's about! That may appear true at times, but it isn't. Even if an artist can't articulate why they do what they do (a surprisingly common phenomenon), there is nonetheless an overarching purpose that governs all genuinely artistic activity. My contention is that this overarching purpose is to give expression to the human condition.

But let's take a step back. In order to express the human condition, the artist draws on his or her creativity. I believe that the creativity of human beings is part of what it means to be made in the image of God. Our God is a creating God, and those in his image are also creators. Sure, some people

---

* This statistic is *not* made up, but it is anecdotal.

may not *feel* particularly creative, but we all create in different ways. We might build things, name things, order things, govern things, shape things, write things, play with things, and so on. All of this is creative in a broad sense. The creativity that artists employ is just one type of human creativity.

Creativity is not an end in itself. It has a purpose—even if some of us are not sure what it is. In the case of the artist, their creativity serves to express the human condition. This can take various forms. Some art expresses a feeling—perhaps something the artist has experienced, or one with which they can empathize. Some art reflects particular life events, whether good or bad. Some art explores the nature of relationships. Some art exists to make people think. Some art intends to offend. Some art underscores our finitude. Some art is simply meant to make us feel good. Some art expresses our connection to God.

One way or another, all these intentions connect to the human condition. That is a gift from God. He has given us the ability to create and experience art as a way to give voice to the things that make us human. We can share, empathize, narrate, explore, reflect, laugh at, and challenge our humanness together. Is it little wonder that no other created being demonstrates such artistic expression? Artistic creativity is uniquely human, and its purpose is to give expression to our humanity.

My point is not that it's possible to *make* a connection between the arts and Jesus. My point is that there already *is* a connection. This is a theological reality. If the arts are a God-given tool to express our humanity, they are necessarily connected to Jesus, because our humanity is connected to him.

We may need to be "creative" in working out how a particular art form expresses our connection to Christ, but finding what's there is easier than inventing something that isn't!

Okay. Now that we agree that there's already a connection between any given art form and Jesus, we need to think through what's going to work in the context of outreach. Let's say you've recognized several points of connection between your art form and Christ. That's great, but you haven't finished yet. Some points of connection might be perfectly valid, offering a wonderful illustration of some profound theological truth. But some points of connection are nevertheless terrible for outreach!

Here's an example. A jazz group consists of individual instrumentalists who play together in such a way that they create a unified and integrated band. They are many, yet they are one. What a lovely illustration of the perichoretic relationships of mutual indwelling within the Godhead! God himself is three persons and yet one God.

Does that one work for you? If so, great, but it's not going to work for your non-Christian neighbor. Pericho *what*? Not every connection between your art form and Christian theology is going to be appropriate for outreach. Not because it's untrue, but because it will not communicate to someone who does not understand theology.

Some artists may struggle to work out which ideas will work and which won't. It's not their fault—they're artists! This is where a partnership between a preacher or pastor and an artist can be helpful. A preacher ought to have a good sense of what will connect with an unbelieving audience, and an artist may reflect on the theological overtones of their craft. Together they will be better placed to find an angle that will enable the communication of Christ through art.

Geoff Deutscher's suggestion led me to develop one of my favorite jazz night talks — *A Jazz Testimonial*. Another pastor, Dave McDonald, suggested I use an idea that I had written about in an article. That suggestion gave birth to the talk I have used more than any other — *Freedom in the Groove*. I've come up with some other talks on my own over the years, but in my opinion these two are the best. And it was a couple of pastors who helped me to realize the evangelistic potential of these ideas.

Professionalism versus Opportunity

It's important to raise two matters that all parties should think through regarding their partnership in arts outreach. While naiveté can be charming, it is usually not helpful. We must think carefully about what we're doing in arts outreach. Two key issues are, first, the tension between professionalism and opportunity, and, second, sorting out false idols.

We begin with professionalism versus opportunity. Artists care about quality. It's part of what makes them an artist. They've spent years of their lives honing their craft through thousands of hours of practice, study, and ruthless self-criticism. Most (normal) people have no idea what it takes to become a truly accomplished artist. A gargantuan level of commitment is required just to be able to play jazz at a professional standard — let alone at a *high* professional standard that stands out among peers. Unless you've done it — or you're an elite athlete, or something similar — you just don't understand. All I can say is: *respect*. An accomplished artist is a special breed whom God has gifted and equipped.

But that's not my point here. The point is that artists care about quality. And you would understand why if you had dedicated thousands of hours of your life to mastering an art form. In fact, for many artists, there is nothing more precious than high quality. It's not about the money (or lack of it, in jazz's case). It's not even about the accolades (or lack of them—you get the picture). For the purist, the greatest reward is the attainment of ever-higher levels of artistry.

So what happens when a hardcore artist partners with a church in an outreach event? I'm generalizing here, but you can expect that the church will primarily be concerned with *people*, while the artist will primarily be concerned with *quality*. As I say, this is a generalization. Plenty of godly Christian artists will have a genuine concern for people, and likewise I know of churches that take quality seriously. The two concerns are not mutually exclusive, but sometimes they can end up in competition.

A common example of this from my own experience arises when churches have wanted to host a jazz night outdoors. The idea is that families can come with their picnic blanket, BBQ chicken, and lemonade, and have a great old time listening to jazz and taking it easy. Not only that, but if it's held, say, in a public park, strangers will just come when they hear the music. That idea might sound good in theory, but not if you're concerned about the quality of the concert. As most musicians know—especially jazz musicians—playing outside is a serious artistic compromise. With few exceptions, outdoor venues tend to have terrible acoustics, and it is very difficult to achieve rapport with the audience.

I've only had a few good experiences of outdoor evangelistic jazz nights, but most have been disasters. So whenever it is presented as an option, I strongly try to dissuade the organizers. Indoors is better if you care about quality. But then again, no strangers are going to walk in off the street if it's an indoor concert, and families can't frolic around on their picnic rug. That's the kind of trade-off that needs to be negotiated.

Another issue that I've dealt with arises when a church has really wanted me to include a member of their church in my band. I can understand why they're asking. What a lovely thing for the church to have one of their own members take part in what's happening. To join the stage with professional musicians. To play for the home crowd. The inevitable question a musician will ask is, "Is Billy good?" And of course, the response will be, "Oh yes, he's great. Everyone thinks so." And in the back of my mind I will be thinking, "Well, 'great' is a relative term. What sounds great to you may not sound so great to me."

After a few bad experiences in the early days, I no longer allow a local musician to join my band. It's just too unpredictable, and it can easily all go bad. The only exception I'll make is if the person is a known player, or if there's a recording I can listen to beforehand—and it sounds *awesome*. A compromise position I have used is to suggest that Billy do a few tunes with his own band before ours takes the stage. Then if it's terrible, at least it won't affect what I'm trying to do. Having said all that, I will admit that in one of my early gigs I played with a local pianist who ended up playing in my band for the next ten years ... but he's the exception, not the rule!

What I want to say to churches is that you need to respect the artistic integrity of whomever you're hoping to partner with in this endeavor. And you need to trust that—generally speaking—the event will be better overall if you allow your artist to do what they do without compromising them in some way. Furthermore, if the event is better, you do a better service to the people at the event. It will be more engaging, more entertaining, more fulfilling, more inspiring, and ultimately more commending of the gospel.

As a musician who has worked with many, many churches over the years doing evangelistic jazz concerts, I tend to turn down opportunities that raise red flags. If I think it's going to be an average experience musically, it's probably not worth doing. Now, some readers will think, "But if it's a gospel opportunity, why turn it down, even if the music is average? Isn't that putting music before Christ?" I understand that concern. And from one point of view, I entirely agree. But there are other factors to consider. For one thing, I need to think about the longevity of what I'm doing. If I do too many "lame" gigs, I won't stay at it for the long term. Musicians know what I'm talking about. Too many uninspiring gigs eventually kill the music within. Once that happens, I'm no good to anyone. So, I'm more careful than I used to be about which invitations I accept, and as a result I'm happy to keep going with this music ministry as long as there is a place for it.

In summary, my solutions to the "artistic" side of this partnership are: I don't play with homegrown musicians ("good" is a relative term); I always bring my own band, consisting of trusted professionals; and the band charges a professional fee. This is first so that I can pay my professional players in a way that will not disadvantage them by taking part in this ministry. Second, it's sometimes a way to ensure that the church will do their job, which is to get people there. It's just human nature to value what you pay for. If we charged nothing, it wouldn't matter to some churches whether or not they managed to make the event work.

Artists of different mediums will need to work out how this looks with respect to their own crafts. Performance artists of various kinds will need to consider factors similar to those mentioned here. Visual artists ought to consider issues that affect the success of an exhibition, such as lighting, appropriate space, exposure, and so on. Whatever the medium, churches need to listen carefully to the artistic concerns of their partnering artists. They know what they're doing, so trust them. Don't assume that your artist is a prima donna because they have artistic "demands" (though that may be the case!); any serious artist is concerned with artistic *integrity*, which is a different thing altogether.

Sorting out False Idols

This is the second matter I need to address. Here I'm speaking primarily to the artist reading this. Just because you're a Christian and you're involved in an artistic event for the sake of the gospel doesn't mean that you'll be immune from ungodly motivations and struggles. I don't know a single Christian musician of high caliber who has not struggled with idolatry at some point in their career. This is a topic I'll address later, but for now I want to raise the following cautions. Just because I've argued above for the importance of artistic integrity and professionalism, this doesn't mean that the event is all about you. It's not. Your motivation for arts-based evangelism must be the glory of God. You shouldn't do it because you can't get any other gigs. The goal of the event is not to advance your career, to impress your fellow artists, or to sell a bunch of merchandise.

I don't struggle with the career thing because I care so little about my musical profile. But my struggle is with classic artistic introspection. Did I play well? Were the tunes hip? Did people catch the nuances in that ballad? Why do they always seem to prefer the drummer? ☺ No. While I'm concerned to offer a professional, high-caliber artistic experience, my ultimate concern must remain the glory of God in evangelism. I should be more concerned about how my gospel talk went than how I played. I should delight in the number of unbelievers present more than the number of albums sold. I should be glad that everyone really engaged with that happening drum solo—grabbing their attention just before the gospel talk—rather than coveting their preference for the drummer.

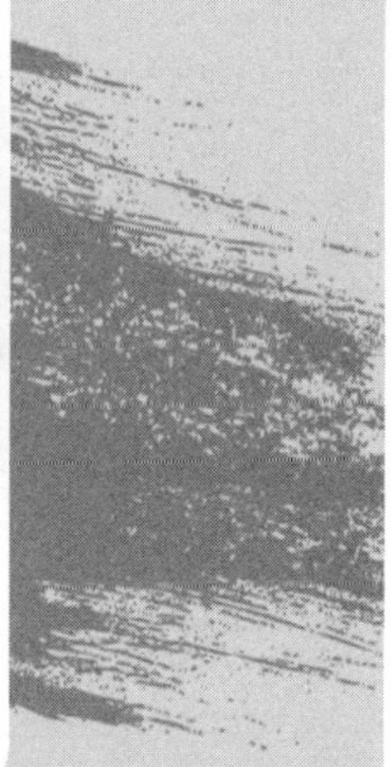

Corrie Ancone

Artist Profile: Richard Maegraith

www.richardmaegraith.com

1. **Describe your artistic interests.**
   I especially love improvised music (jazz music, in particular), although I'm constantly discovering new music and genres that are opening my ears up. I'm also into the visual arts, especially the genre of Impressionism, and Australian Impressionism in particular.

2. **What struggles have you had as a Christian engaged with the arts?**
   Artists of all genres deal in gray. Christians (especially Western evangelicals) often deal in black and white.

And fair enough, on one level, we have a black-and-white gospel (John 14:6). Trust in Jesus and be saved; reject the Son and forfeit life (John 3:36). However, there is much within our faith that is gray and paradoxical (and let's face it, completely "out of this world"), and this can be an area in which the Christian artistic community can use their gifts. To teach, encourage, and captivate the non-artsy mainstream church and reach unbelievers with the gospel.

So, the struggle can come when dealing in gray artistically can start to influence the non-gray doctrines that evangelical Christians hold. Maybe Jesus isn't the only way to the Father—after all, no *one* genre of music has a monopoly on beauty or truth. How can Christians enforce their views so dogmatically when we can be enriched so much through other cultures and their artistic traditions? Most cultures and people groups have wonderful music and dancing—often inspired by their ancient and sacred texts; how then can Christians claim to have the truth as only taught in the Bible? That seems pretty bigoted. And so on. So there are struggles with ideologies and worldviews affecting one's theology. This is a big area for the artist. Syncretism can arise out of these struggles.

Other struggles I've had with the arts include knowing when to cut ties with certain secular musicians and artists as a result of the "edgy" and sometimes sinful nature of some content and performances—the classic "being in the world, but not of it" dilemma. I think this is potentially the biggest struggle for Christian artists and musicians. Taking opportunities to perform and network, but eventually being faced with the choice of becoming a part of the world to enhance one's career, and so on—or making a stand for Christ and losing face and gigs. I've had to say no to a few bands and gigs because of who my Lord is, and it's a tough call when you're on a freelance income and you're only as good as your last (often, low-paying) gig.

Also, the lifestyle of an artist doesn't fit in well with most churches. On a Sunday morning, 9:30 is recovery sleep-in time from the late Saturday night gig, Sunday evening is gig time, Wednesday night Bible study is often a gig or teaching opportunity, and church weekend camps are always a disaster for a person who makes money on the weekend! What happens, therefore, is that Christians start hanging out more with their secular musician friends (who share the same hours and similar musical interests) and less with their Christian friends, and so they slide into disbelief (or nominalism) as they leave regular fellowship.

Meanwhile, it seems, few churches and Christians are mature and Christlike enough to follow up these people and get alongside them outside of church meeting times. They are almost condemned for not being "regular" at church or "disciplined" to be there. I've seen this happen so often, and it's a great grief to me. Never mind that the same people are often highly sought after to play in the church music team. But don't get me started on church music and its relationship to the artist!

3. Describe the ministry you've been able to have through the arts.

As a result of the struggles discussed above and the subsequent opportunities to proclaim the gospel, I've been privileged to be involved in ministry to and with musicians for the last few years. I began a thing in 2007 called the Muso Hang. We started by meeting in a restaurant in Surry Hills, and we'd read the Bible and pray for one another, then walk up the road and see a gig together at a pub. We'd pray for opportunities to talk of Jesus. This eventually turned into bimonthly gatherings in my family home. We'd invite Christian musicians and other musicians to come and hang, jam, eat and drink, and hear a talk from the Bible. Sometimes we'd have a discussion time after the talk. I think it was popular because it afforded a certain amount of anonymity and no commitment for those who just wanted to check it out.

This idea led to the planting of Freedom of the Artist Church, Marrickville, in January 2011. This church meets on a Monday afternoon (the unofficial Sabbath for musicians), and currently consists of improvised musical accompaniment of Psalms and apocalyptic Scripture from the Bible. I also take secular songs (for example, Joni Mitchell's "A Case of You") and compare and contrast the themes of the song with biblical stories and texts (in this case, John 4). We pray for each other and have afternoon tea together. It's very informal.

Another strategy for my ministry is to be in a number of secular bands and pray that God uses me to proclaim and witness to Christ in those relationships.

4. Concerning other artists you know, what is the single biggest barrier stopping them from coming to Christ?

I don't claim to know the answer to this. However, I'd say that for many artists in Sydney, it's just that they don't have any or many Christian networks or friends. They are "unreached," as the missiologists say. They are a people group, and they're completely under the radar of mainstream Christianity. So we need more Christian artists and musicians who are in the industry for the kingdom, not their own glory. They only hear about Jesus and the gospel if they have someone they trust and respect to preach it to them.

Keeley Manca Lambert

photography by: Alissa Noelle Photography

Richard Maegraith

photography by: Corrie Ancone

Dan McGowan

photography by: © 2012 John Nimmo

Kristin Berardi

photography by: Karen Steins

Hayley Neal

photography by: David Elsey

Ian McGilvray

Beauty Retold

Artwork by: Ian McGilvray

Lucy

Artwork by: Ian McGilvray

Keith Birchley

photography by: Karl Birchley

Con Campbell

photography by: Bronwyn Campbell

Con Campbell

photography by: Steb Fisher Photography

www.steb.com.au

CHAPTER 3

WHAT WORKS AND WHY

It took a while for me to work out what works in an evangelistic jazz concert, and even longer to fine-tune those things. Like an artist's craft itself, an arts-based outreach event requires careful, self-critical reflection. Especially if this is something to be repeated for various churches, the artist must be willing to reinvent their "show" rather than just repeat old routines that may or may not work.

I'm a pretty harsh self-critic, but there are still things I don't notice that can be improved. I've learned the value of listening to the critique of others. Of course, this always needs to be evaluated — because sometimes you *are* right! — but a humble acceptance of the opinion of others can go a long way. One thing that took me a while to get right is how "hardcore" my jazz concerts would be. Sure, I don't want to compromise artistic integrity, but let's face it, there is a way to play jazz that will connect with those who are not jazz afficionados and there's a way to alienate them. In the early days, I could sometimes alienate my audience because I wasn't thinking enough about accessibility.

My dear friend, and aforementioned drummer, John Morrison, has helped over the years with this. I remember him subtly saying things like, "Remember this is not a jazz audience, man." Or, "Do we wanna play something they'll know?" Or, "Your solos are great man, but maybe they could be a bit shorter—just thinking of the audience!" Of course, he was right. And I started working out how to maintain artistic integrity while choosing tunes that some listeners might know, tunes that were easy to listen to, and keeping solos short(ish). After all, Charlie Parker played short solos, and no one is a more serious jazz musician than Bird! You can't buy advice like that, and our jazz nights have been much better for it.

Another thing that works is to explain what you're doing. Most evangelistic jazz concert audiences do not really know jazz (especially in Australia, but even in America). One of the best things I can do is explain a little about jazz—how it works, what it's about, and why we love it. This is not the kind of thing Miles Davis would do (just talking to the audience could be a step too far for him!), but think of it as an artist in education mode. Be an ambassador for your art. Help people to like it and appreciate it. Don't leave them in the dark.

Something to avoid by all means is the old "bait and switch" technique, which sadly I have fallen into on occasion. The way this might work with a jazz night is to invite people to a concert but not tell them ahead of time that there will be Christian content. So the concert is going just fine—the first set is funny and informative with good music; everyone's having a good time. And then—clang!—out of nowhere there's all this Jesus stuff. Churches and their people really *must* be up front that the event to which they are inviting people will have some sort of message about Jesus. Sometimes churches consult with me about a poster or postcards they're designing in order to invite people to the concert. I always insist that it is made clear that it will be a Christian event and therefore will have some Christian content. I don't mind how they say it, and it doesn't need to be particularly descriptive, but the last thing I want is for people to show up who are then surprised, and perhaps even aggravated, that it was all an elaborate "trap" to sneak in some Jesus talk. We have to be up front about what we're doing.

In addition, I always ask the MC to begin the concert with a brief acknowledgment that I will be saying something about Jesus later in the night. By all means, make it funny if you like: "Con is going to talk about jazz tonight, and later, as a Christian, he's going to explain what jazz has to do with Jesus. That ought to be interesting, since they don't seem to be connected at all!" Fine by me; we just need *something* said to kick things off. Then, when the Jesus content comes, it's not out of the blue and there is no bait and switch.

Setting Appropriate Goals

As with any endeavor, it's important to set appropriate goals. Christians can sometimes set unrealistically high goals for their evangelistic events. Of course, God is sovereign and will bring his elect to himself at his appointed time, but on the whole it seems to me that the day of Billy Graham-type crusades is over—at least for now. Yes, people still come to Christ through evangelistic events, but Western societies are less Christianized than they were in Billy Graham's era. Unbelievers are a step or two "further away" in their understanding and willingness to approach God than the unbelievers of fifty or sixty years ago.

There is still an important place for outreach events in our evangelistic strategies, but these will tend to be one part of a sequence of steps toward Christ. We may not see as many unbelievers "cross the line" at an event compared to the 1950s—and we may not use an altar call—but an event can nonetheless help an unbeliever on their ongoing journey toward understanding the gospel and conversion.

This reality has caused me to think carefully about what is realistic (under God) for something like an evangelistic jazz night. I don't know this as fact, but I suspect that no one has been converted "on the spot" at any of my 250 evangelistic jazz nights. That's okay with me, because that's not really what I'm aiming at. The wide appeal of arts-based events means that they will attract lots of totally unchurched people. Again, it is generally unrealistic to expect that such people will be converted through their *first* Christian contact. Realizing who my audience is means that I can help set the sequence in motion.

I think of my jazz nights as a "first date." What's the purpose of a first date? To get a second date, of course! I want people to have a wonderful first contact with Christianity. I want them to hear the gospel, have some fun, meet some Christian people, and leave feeling good about the whole thing. I want them to be willing to go to the next outreach event, or perhaps go to church on Sunday, as a result of their first encounter with Christianity.

I know of people who have come to Christ in exactly this way. A few years ago, at a jazz night at a large church in Sydney, a man enthusiastically introduced himself to me. This man had been an active member of the church with his family for the previous three or four years and was a delightful Christian man. He told me that the first time he had ever walked into a church was at the jazz night I had performed at that same church five years earlier. That was his first contact with Christianity. As a result of that first jazz night, he went along to church the following Sunday. After a year or so, he had become a Christian. Sure, he wasn't converted through my jazz night, but it was an important first step along the way. I thank God for the privilege of being involved in his journey toward Christ. And that man is who I have in mind when I think about the "target" of a jazz night. I hope and pray that through their first contact with the gospel, many others will begin down the same road.

That's a pretty realistic goal for arts-based outreach. The wide appeal of the arts means that we will attract a high number of people who are completely unchurched. What a wonderful opportunity! So, set appropriate goals with your events. Aim for a great first date. Aim to spark someone's interest to find out more. Aim to provide an overwhelmingly positive experience of Christianity. Aim to move someone one step along the way. Aim for a second date.

Working Together

Let me conclude this chapter with some thoughts for both the artist and the host church on working together for a successful event. I've found that an essential ingredient for an arts-based outreach event is rapport. I would argue that the level of rapport between the artist/artists and the audience has more potential to ensure success or derail the event than almost anything else. You might have the most brilliant evangelistic talk lined up, but if your audience is not warm toward you, it will not land.

Remember, if a good percentage of your audience is unchurched, there will be lots of emotional, intellectual, and spiritual barriers to get over before the gospel is properly heard. Unbelievers are not as a positively predisposed to giving you a good hearing as they may have been generations ago. Many will come with some kind of skepticism in place—perhaps with some unhelpful stereotypes of what Christians are like. We need to get past those barriers, and rapport is key.

But rapport is not the artist's responsibility alone. The partnering church has a lot to do with it too. My band works hard at developing rapport; we explain how jazz works, we include a lot of humor, and we share ourselves in various ways. All of this builds rapport, and the rapport serves a single function: to provide a context in which I can give an evangelistic talk. Since I spend the whole first set talking between tunes, engaging the audience with information, it does not feel unnatural to keep talking in the second set, but this time about the gospel. They're used to me talking. They're used to me explaining things they don't yet understand. They're even used to me making a soft sell—in the first set, I'm selling jazz; in the second, I'm selling the gospel!

The artist needs to work at these things, translated into one's own art form as appropriate. For the visual artist, for example, rapport might be achieved by talking through one's process, inspiration, or struggle in creating their work. But the host church needs to be conscious of this goal too. I can't tell you the number of times that my "rapport project" has been derailed by the thoughtless organization, preparation, or just dodgy presentation skills of various churches. If a church wants to host a successful arts-based event, they must think the rapport-factor through carefully, and there are several elements to consider.

Speaking again from a jazz concert perspective, here are some ways that a church can wreck it. The space might be terrible; have you considered the acoustics? Do you really need to hold the event outside? How conducive is the place to a jazz concert? The seating arrangement might be unhelpful. Why set up seats with their backs to the stage? Why is the first row of seats ten meters away from the band? Is "portrait" the best format for the room? Have you considered "landscape"? You might have created the dreaded "jazz-as-background-music vibe." Must you serve food while the band is playing? Have you thought about how to set the artist up properly? Have you considered how to communicate that the event is a "concert" rather than "background music"? Have you somehow encouraged people to talk through the show? The MC might be terrible. Will the MC create rapport, getting the process going for the artist, or make it harder to win people over? Has the MC even bothered to check with the artist regarding what is helpful to do and say?

Neither the artist nor the church can assume anything. Both parties need to *talk*! As an artist I am constantly amazed at things that churches do not take care of—things that seem obvious to me. But I guess these things are obvious to me because I've been doing this for a long time. A church might be completely new at this kind of thing, and if I *assume* the things that I take to be obvious, then it's my own fault when things go pear-shaped. And let me tell you, they *can* go pear-shaped! There are generally two recipes for disaster in my experience. The first is forgetting to communicate with the partnering church. The second is the church's decision to ignore the artist's advice.

Let me finish with an unpleasant example of the latter recipe for disaster. A Christian university group booked me to play on campus. They asked if it would work to do my thing in the university bar. I commented that it had worked on other campuses to play the university bar, but only if the group controlled the venue. It would only work if the Christian group had booked the room for the night. This particular group didn't want to do that; they figured they'd rather have the bar open as usual to anyone, in order to reach a wider group of people. There would be lots of people at the bar, playing pool, or whatever, and they wanted to evangelize such folk. I could sympathize with the motivation. But I strongly objected, explaining that my jazz night depended on creating rapport, having a captive audience, and certainly not "preaching against their will"!

But the Christian university group insisted it would be okay to do it their way. I reluctantly gave in. In retrospect, I should have pulled out of the event. It was a complete disaster. Forget about rapport. People were talking at the bar, playing pool, making out, whatever — and all were completely ignoring the band, except the little group of Christians who were hosting the night. When I tried to speak in between tunes, I could barely be heard above the racket. As the talk approached, I began to be overtaken with dread as I anticipated the train wreck around the corner.

Sure enough, it was a train wreck! I was trying to share the gospel over the top of the noise of the room. No one was listening (except the Christians). And I was heckled! Some guy playing pool objected to me speaking to them about Jesus. Whenever I said "Jesus," he called out "Jesus! Jesus!" (imagine a mocking tone). It was awful. It was easily my worst experience of public evangelism, and on the plane home I came close to quitting altogether. What a disaster. Artists—don't let that be you! Churches—don't let that happen on your watch!

© 2012 John Nimmo

Artist Profile: Dan McGowan

www.danmcgowan.com

1. Describe your artistic interests.
   I primarily work as a comedian with content that is clean. This makes me a suitable entertainer for church and Christian events, corporate events, and most community events. I also offer professional business presentations on various topics, and I work freelance as an on-camera actor, voice-over talent, writer, and musician.

2. What struggles have you had as a Christian engaged with the arts?
   I've actually had struggles in both the secular and sacred worlds, which initially surprised me. On the

secular side my initial struggles were simply learning how to engage and nurture relationships with "non-believers" whose values, morals, and other areas simply were not what I agree with. But over time I've come to value these relationships because, at their heart, they are honest—and I appreciate that.

In Christian circles I have struggled with a lack of vision for "the arts" as a viable means of communicating the gospel and offering clean entertainment options to those who continue to complain about the lack of clean entertainment coming out of Hollywood, for example. There also tends to be an "it's your ministry" mind-set among many churches who are simply not willing to financially support the entertainment abilities of those gifted in this area. As someone who served in churches for over twenty-five years, I know very well that budgets are tight. However, I also believe that a "worker is worthy of his wage" and wish churches could expand their vision in this area.

3. Describe the ministry you've been able to have through the arts.

One thing I never expected was to have opportunities to share in deep, spiritual conversations with people after corporate (nonchurch) events. This has happened many times, usually after everyone else has left. I value such opportunities. Also, I have had amazing opportunities to get to know other comedians who are not believers — and simply form great friendships! Out of those friendships I've experienced conversations that I know have impacted me and the other person in potentially life-transforming ways. Very exciting!

4. Concerning other artists you know, what is the single biggest barrier stopping them from coming to Christ?

Well, this sounds like a loaded question, but I'll do my best! Ha! I think far too many Christians feel the need to live life in a legalistic manner. In other words, if we step over *any* line that is "inappropriate," then it impacts our salvation. Such legalism can become a barrier that prevents unbelievers from coming to Jesus. I see many people who *first* need to be loved and accepted before we challenge them with deeper kingdom issues. I have found that the more I show love and acceptance, the wider the door opens for further discussion on spiritual levels. Not to sound cliché, but — *what would Jesus do?*

CHAPTER 4

OUTREACH *THROUGH* THE ARTS

In the previous two chapters, I explored issues involved in churches partnering with artists in outreach. There are things for both parties to think about, and the communication of expectations and goals between the two is an important ingredient for success in such endeavors. In this chapter, I want to take a step back from that to consider differing ways in which an artist can utilize their specific art form for evangelism. The model assumed in the previous two chapters is not the only valid option, and there are at least two ways to look at this whole issue. I summarize these approaches as "the message and the medium" and "the medium and the message." Let me unpack what I mean by these two phrases.

The Message and the Medium

When I speak of the message and the medium, the order of those two elements is significant. This kind of arts-based outreach gives priority to the *message* rather than the medium, and it sees the latter as a servant of the former. This is the kind of outreach that has been the topic thus far, illustrated through my experience with evangelistic jazz nights. In thinking about jazz nights, the required preparation, the importance of rapport, the communication between artist and church, and so on, the focus has been on using jazz as a vehicle for the gospel message.

With this kind of outreach, the vehicle is ultimately not that important. Sure, it's important to me as an artist, as it will be for any artist, but it is basically a tool to be used in service of a higher purpose. The artistic medium provides an opportunity to speak a message. It provides a connection, a context, a reason to stand up in front of people and address them. The medium does all that, but the medium is not what it's all for. That's why I can generalize principles from jazz nights to any kind of arts-based outreach; the art form itself is not intrinsic to the outreach. Any art form can achieve much the same thing. In a jazz night, there is nothing special about jazz that is required to speak the gospel; it's just a vehicle that I happen to have at my disposal.

Several years ago I was interviewed for a special program aired by Australia's ABC Radio National. The topic was jazz and spirituality. All kinds of musicians were interviewed, and most of them tried to claim that their spiritual connection to God was somehow mediated through their music. I was the odd one out because I strongly denied this idea. Jesus Christ is the only mediator between God and human beings, and I refused to say that through playing jazz I drew nearer to God or something like that.

When the radio program aired, I came under mild criticism for "using" jazz to preach the gospel. An academic from the Macquarie University, who had been doing some research on Australian jazz musicians and spirituality, actually used these words of me: "In a live situation Con's had the ability to build up a rapport with the audience, to create a relationship with them that enables him to then deliver this sermon and have it received more relationally and favourably as a result, rather than just kind of hitting people with his strong gospel message." Well, the academic meant it as a criticism, but I took it as a compliment! Of course that's what I was doing, and I have good reason. Jazz is a great vehicle for outreach, but I'm not going to pretend it's more powerful than that. It just isn't. People are not going to come into Jesus' kingdom because I played an especially pretty ballad. That's not how it works. The New Testament teaches us that repentance and belief in Christ occurs through the proclamation of the *gospel*. The message must be heard for anything to happen.

Thus, putting the message before the medium is a good thing to do as a Christian artist. After all, I'm a *Christian* artist, not an artist who happens to be a Christian. We must be defined first by Christ before other things define us. If this is the case, it will be easy—even for the most hardcore purist—to put the message ahead of the medium. Having said that, however, there is also a place for *the medium and the message*, when the focus is actually on the medium rather than the message. It's to this idea we now turn.

The Medium and the Message

It's not wrong to put it the other way around, so that the medium comes before the message. It depends on the context and the purpose. Christians can perform music or create artistic works that are *informed* by the message of Christ, without necessarily being explicitly gospel-*announcing*. In such cases, the message may be woven into the medium somehow. Perhaps the lyrics of a song can point to Christ in a gentle way, or they can explore the Christian experience of life. Perhaps a painting is inspired by an Isaianic prophecy. Perhaps a sculpture depicts a world without God. I've known Christian artists who have endeavored to achieve exactly these aims through their art form. Their Christian worldview cannot help but shape their creations, and it provides inspiration for their creativity.

There are strengths and weaknesses to this "medium and message" approach. First, some weaknesses. Such an approach is necessarily less explicit in its gospel content. Obviously this will be the case if there is no preaching involved. Thus, it is even more unlikely that people will be converted through such artistic projects. In fact, it is probably impossible for such to happen, if there is no explicit gospel content. Some people, therefore, might prefer to call this "pre-evangelism."

The implicit nature of this approach means that any "meaning" intended for the work will be open for interpretation. I remember when my friend Adam Chessum was a student at the Canberra School of Art. He had created a wonderful painting inspired by Isaiah 53. For him, its purpose and meaning were clear: it pointed to Christ as the Suffering Servant of Isaiah. The painting's tones and hues, shapes and contours all served this intended meaning.

But I found it amusing when Adam reported to me his frustration as he shared the work in class with his lecturer and fellow students. Each student took a moment to introduce his or her piece, before the class would discuss the work, its technical merit, and its meaning. Adam explained that he had been inspired by the magnificent prophecy of Isaiah 53, and how the painting's features all served this inspiration. But when the class discussion ensued, the meaning of the painting was all of a sudden up for grabs. Each student interpreted it differently, stating what the painting meant for them and how it informs their own experience of the world. Adam was not happy! But through that experience he (and I) learned that nonexplicit art forms are limited in their proclamation value, since they can be misinterpreted. There's nothing wrong with producing such works—of course not!—but there is only so much that can be done if outreach is your goal.

But there are strengths inherent to a "medium and message" approach. For one thing, such art will normally seem more credible to the art world. If you're not using your art simply as a vehicle to preach but have allowed it to be shaped by an important source of inspiration, it becomes part of the pantheon of artistic endeavor, all of which is inspired by something. Art created through a "medium and message" approach will receive a wider audience in the art scene itself, because it will be seen as "genuine" art.

On the radio program I mentioned above, this was evident in the way in which the great Australian Christian jazz group

Selah was treated.* *Selah* consists of Christian jazz musicians who share together as brothers and sisters in Christ and are inspired by their common Lord. The music is "Christian" in its lyrics and inspiration, but the message is simply woven into the fabric of the music itself. For the jazz critic, this is authentic music because it is inspired and shaped by the musicians' beliefs rather than simply providing a vehicle for their message. The advantage of this is that their music is accepted in "secular" venues and radio stations. Sure, people know it's Christian, but it's not "preachy"; it's just art. And very good art.

During the last few years I've been involved in a band with similar goals. *Transit* is a jazz group of Christians, and we play Christ-inspired music, some of which includes modern jazz arrangements of classic hymns. It's clear by the titles of the tunes that the group is shaped by our Christian identity. But we have no vocalist in the group; it's purely instrumental music. And that means there is no explicit message—not even through lyrics. We have no lyrics! But the great thing about this has been that we are able to perform in all kinds of secular venues, and our album has received airplay on secular radio stations.

We know that no one is going to get converted by listening to *Transit*, but that's not the point. The band gives us an opportunity to be Christians in the secular jazz scene in a way that identifies who we are to others, but it does not ram our message down their throats. We know that, at least, there is some identifiable Christian shape to our secular performances. When we discuss what some of the tunes are about and announce their titles, we hope that this will create talking points and will be somewhat thought provoking.

---

* Not to be confused with the well-known American group of the same name.

This approach certainly has a place and ought to be encouraged. But there's no denying that it is ultimately less useful for *outreach* compared to the "message and medium" approach. My preferred option is to take both approaches! I feel most satisfied as an artist and as a preacher when *Transit* performs at an outreach event. We get to play great artistically satisfying music that is Christ-inspired, and there is also explicit gospel content through the sermon. Those are special occasions.

I think the Christian artist needs to work out how God has gifted them. Can you preach? Are you able to articulate the gospel in a clear and winsome manner? Does the idea of weaving the message of Christ into a performance or artistic creation excite you? Perhaps it terrifies you, or, perhaps, repulses you. Work out what you're comfortable doing. Of course, it's good to be open to challenge and to try things that might not seem quite right initially. If I had not done that, I wouldn't be writing this book!

But once you've tried things out in various ways, it's worth reflecting on what you think God has wired you to do in this regard. It's interesting hearing Kristin Berardi's reflections on this issue in her artist profile (below). Working out what God would have her do with her music was clearly a struggle for her, but she has come to the conclusion (and rightly so, I think) that God has wired her to perform in the secular jazz scene. Her listeners and fellow musicians know she is a Christian, and her presence in the jazz world gives her opportunities to speak of Jesus. Given her high profile in Australia and internationally, and the respect with which her artistry is regarded, she is a lovely witness to Christ in a very unchristian subculture.

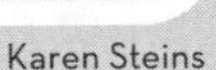
Karen Steins

Artist Profile: Kristin Berardi

www.kristinberardi.com

1. **Describe your artistic interests.**
   Music and photography. I am a musician by trade—it's my "job," but I feel blessed to love doing it, to love practicing it and needing it in my life. I am a jazz singer and enjoy what that music allows—the freedom to improvise and interact with fellow musicians, making each gig unique and hopefully in the moment. I also teach jazz singing at universities in Australia as a guest lecturer, and I am on staff at the Australian National University in Canberra. I also teach singing and beginner piano from home. Photography is just my hobby.

2. What struggles have you had as a Christian engaged with the arts?

I found it difficult living in a smaller community early on, as there were few fellow Christians in my field. Not that I was made to feel uncomfortable by others, but I would have been very encouraged if there had been more than two of us in the Jazz Department at the Conservatorium.

The thing I have struggled with most, I think, is that I perform "secular" music, not Christian music, and I have felt torn about spending my time investing in this jazz genre while wondering whether I should be leading the singing in church or writing solely Christian tunes. I have spent much time talking to God about this, and over time I have realized that he calls us to our own path. But I must admit, I sometimes struggle with this even now. I just keep talking to God and making sure I'm on the path he wants. That's the thing to keep in check, as his requirements of me may change. But for now I feel I am doing what I am meant to.

3. Describe the ministry you've been able to have through the arts.

I have been put in certain situations in which I've been able to talk with others wrestling with the same questions (about secular and Christian music). I have encouraged them to talk to God and follow his leading and guidance. I know my gifting is not to lead church worship (as I tend to lead them astray!), though I can occasionally perform a piece to worship him. But my calling is to perform my own music and jazz standards in performance settings, and to pray for his anointing over my voice so that people will be touched by him, will think on him, and will give him the glory. I am so thankful for this as I have seen him work time and time again — it gives greater purpose to what I am doing and allows me to give it over to him. I know I am just the vessel and it is definitely all him.

I have had people come up to me at gigs, wanting to talk about God. Or they may say, "That voice is a gift from God," even when some of them — I know — do not believe in him. He certainly works in amazing and incredible ways when we yield ourselves and our endeavors to him. Also, I believe that we won't always know how he works, but I know that if I pray over the gig or the situation, I am always calmer and much more able to deliver the music in the way I desire — all praise to him.

4. Concerning other artists you know, what is the single biggest barrier stopping them from coming to Christ?

The biggest barrier people admit to is "church." However, I'm not so sure it's that simple. I think other factors are often at play. I have heard many people say that they wouldn't want to step foot in a church, having had a bad experience when younger. I find a lot of people seem to forget that other people can falter and cause hurt and pain, and that Christians are in that boat too. But that seems to put people off Christianity a lot—or perhaps it's just another barrier that Satan uses to keep people away from the Truth.

I think that for many artists the idea that they must follow doctrine is off-putting, and yet we all know that a sporting match needs rules, boundaries, and standards to be really great and challenging and to run smoothly.

In Australia we are happy to live in the gray areas, being put off by things "spiritual," perhaps fearing what others will think of us. I find that artists are quite accepting of others and their beliefs in general. However, they seem also to be more interested in choosing what they like from various religious practices, perhaps combining them to "make their own" spirituality to live by.

CHAPTER 5

OUTREACH *TO* THE ARTS

Up to this point we have been concerned with arts-based outreach. This chapter and the next two are about evangelism that *targets* the arts—that is, outreach to unbelieving artists and artistic communities. This is a complicated mission with many challenges, primarily because artists tend to form their own subcultures within our communities. We will explore the nature of such subcultures, various ways in which it is possible to reach into such groups, and some of the reasons for which every church ought to take it seriously.

Subcultures

To the uninitiated, it may seem strange to claim that artists normally live within their own artistic subcultures. Such a claim may sound odd because, on the surface, artists often appear to be normal, well-adjusted members of the community. And often they are! (And often they are not!) Whether or not they appear this way, serious artists nevertheless are generally best regarded as a different breed.

Let's think about the factors that shape a subculture. First, there's language. Do artists speak their own language? You bet they do! Or, at least, they speak a distinct dialect. Sure, many fields of specialization come complete with their own jargon and technical terms. But that's not what I'm talking about. Yes, there is jargon and technical vocabulary that artists will share within their own discipline. But in addition to this, artists tend to have their own *way of speaking* that permeates their entire speech, not just discussions about art.

The jazz subculture is the one I know best, and it is patently obvious that jazz musicians share a common way of speaking. I defy any non-jazz person to interpret the following sentence: "'Man, great chops; your axe really cuts the changes." How do you go with that one?

Let me parse it for you. "Man": it's not unique to jazz musicians, of course, but this form of address is virtually universal among jazz speakers, and it covers men *and* women! This is particularly noticeable in Australia, since nearly everyone else uses the word "mate." Some jazzers say "mate," but only when they're trying to be cross-cultural; "man" is the word to use when a jazzer is being true to the tribe. When I became a Christian, I had to get comfortable calling people "mate," since that's what Australian Christians say. I now use "mate" for Christian friends and "man" for jazz friends.

"Great chops": this is a compliment (you could probably tell that much) about one's technical ability on an instrument. "Chops" is standard jazz vocabulary for technique, control, mastery. It's normally used with reference to an instrument, but it is often used for "normal" speech too and can refer to anyone's technical ability at anything. To say, "That dude has some serious chops," when referring to a physicist, means that he really knows what he's talking about.

"Your axe": an axe is an instrument. It could be a piano or a double bass, a saxophone or a xylophone. It doesn't matter. An axe is what you use to *cut*.

"Cuts the changes": This refers to negotiating the chord progression of a tune during an improvisation. "Changes" is just shorthand for "chord changes" (= chord progression). To "cut" the changes means that a musician can play freely, creatively, accurately, and with "chops" through the changes.

Okay, so this example is pretty jargony and deals with musical entities. But every word in that sentence can be used by a jazz musician to speak of nonmusical things. In other words, the music jargon is extrapolated into general speech, understood only by other speakers of the language. My wife can always tell when I'm on the phone with another jazz musician. I speak differently. I'm speaking to my people.

Language defines a subculture, but there are other elements that do this too. People in certain subcultures tend to live together. This is often true of artists. They share houses with other artists and like to live in artistic neighborhoods. Not only are such neighborhoods "hip" in their subculture, but artists like to be around other artists. This is so they can hang out, jam together (if musicians), paint together, write together, and so on.

Lots of musicians I know *only* hang out with other musicians. Apart from family, some artists only have friendships with other artists. There are at least two reasons for this. First, artists can get tired of people who "don't understand them," so prefer to be with those who do. Other friends and acquaintances drop off. And second, their lifestyle facilitates it. Some jazz guys I know are never out of bed before 1:00 p.m., and are never in bed before 3:00 a.m. If you basically live at *night*, there is a large portion of mainstream society that you will never have any contact with. That is, most of society! Who else is out at 2:00 a.m. on a weeknight? Every weeknight?

Artists live differently in other ways too. This is a gross generalization, but on the whole artists tend to adopt looser systems of morality. Their attitude to sex, drugs, and alcohol is frequently stereotyped by the mainstream—and for good reason. It's generally true! They often resist routine, structure, and organization. An organized artist is a rare breed indeed and will invite suspicion from "more genuine" artistic types. Artists just live in a different world with different rules (or no rules). That's partly why they love being an artist. And it's why mainstream culture is so fascinated by them—either wanting to be like them, or wishing they'd go "get a real job."

My point in saying all this is to demonstrate that artists really do belong to subcultures of their own, and this has implications for outreach. For one thing, many artistic communities are best regarded as "unreached people groups." Since artists often only spend time with other artists, and if there are no Christians in a particular artistic subculture, those artists will not know any Christians at all. There will be no evangelism taking place among them, and they will have no exposure to the gospel. Since the best evangelism occurs through relationships, this is all but impossible in a subculture without Christians in it.

Reaching a Subculture

As someone who is interested in outreach to artists, it's good that I can talk the talk, and I can play. I understand the jazz subculture as a "native," since I have come up through it. I get its values and its ideals. But my problem these days is that I don't live in that subculture anymore. I'm like an expat; I can visit, speak the language, and engage with the culture, but I live elsewhere. I spend most of my time hanging around the world of theological education and churches, which might as well be another country. I still play gigs, go out to listen to gigs, and spend time with jazz friends, so I haven't forgotten my roots. But at the same time, I'm not right in there as I once was. All that means is that I have the tools for outreach into the jazz subculture, but my reach is fairly limited.

By contrast, my good friend Richard Maegraith, whom I profiled earlier, has managed to keep one foot in the jazz subculture and the other in Christian ministry. In fact, he works half time in ministry and half time as a professional musician. He's a gifted evangelist in any case, but his reach into the Sydney jazz community is far more effective than mine because he's remained fully engaged with it. All the jazz cats (= musicians) know that Richard is a serious Christian, and probably half of them have been evangelized by him at some point. But the fact that he is a highly respected saxophonist—one of Sydney's best—gives him significant credibility among musicians. He's one of them, yet he's a Christian. He belongs to the jazz community and so is able to shine Christ's light into that dark place.

Richard's success as an evangelist to the Sydney jazz world depends most of all on his credibility. It's great to be able to speak the language and understand the culture and so on, but the respect with which he's held is founded on his artistic credibility. The reality is that artistic subcultures of all kinds — not just jazz — operate as meritocracies. Those artists with the greatest skill become the leaders of their tribe.

It's a fascinating phenomenon to observe. Some guys, who by any other standard would not be regarded as cool or popular, are treated as gods because they play great. It doesn't matter how socially awkward they might be, or how good looking (or not!) they might be; what matters is how they play, and if they play great, they go straight to the top of the heap. By the same token, if you don't play that great, you will find yourself somewhere further down the pecking order. Again, it doesn't matter if you are clever, articulate, good-looking, funny, or whatever; if you can't play, you got nothing!

This means that the most effective people for outreach into artistic communities are fellow artists. And the more artistic credibility they have, the better. If your church is interested in outreach to the arts, your first step ought to be to find a committed believing artist who has a passport into that people group. The other way to think about it is this: if you find yourself with an artist or artists in your fellowship, you have an opportunity to tap into a mission field.

Two Kinds of Missionaries

So does that mean that artistic subcultures are totally closed to all non-artists? Not exactly. In fact, artists can develop great respect for nonartists. A musician will respect a devoted music lover, for example. The music lover might not play at all, but can access the music community through their knowledge of music, patronage of the arts, or even just through a fascination with and delight for artistic creativity. Such people can in fact become very dear to artists. The key here, however, is not to pass yourself off as an artist if, in fact, you are not one.

While musicians can respect an appreciative nonmusician, they will find it difficult to respect a bad musician. Remember, it's a meritocracy; a musician who doesn't play well is at the lowest rank of all. For musicians there is a difference between a "musician" and "someone who plays music." There's all the difference in the world. If you play a bit of guitar on Sundays at your church, the worst thing you could do to engage a real musician is to pretend you're doing the same thing. You're not. Trust me, you're just not. If you don't play at a professional standard, don't call yourself a musician when you're with musicians. You'll be better off in the category of "nonmusician."

Thus there are two kinds of missionaries into artistic communities; both depend on the currency of credibility. The first, and most effective, is the believing artist. He or she can access that world as a born-and-bred native, speaking the language and relating to other artists naturally and authentically. The second is the Christian with an interest in the arts. This person can engage with artists in relationships of mutual respect. While this second kind of missionary will not have the same reach or penetration into an artistic community as the first, some genuine engagement *is* possible. Once believers have access to artistic subcultures, they are free to speak the gospel into those worlds. The nature of such evangelism is the topic of the next two chapters.

personal

Artist Profile: Ian McGilvray

1. **Describe your artistic interests.**

Since I was a kid, I have always loved to paint and draw. Painting and drawing have been for me natural ways of exploring the world around me, pondering and celebrating the wonder of the natural world and of people. For many years, making visual art was relegated to the occasional weekend or holiday—more of a side interest. In recent years, however, I have taken up visual art as a calling and a career in lieu of my previous job as an architect.

My favored subject is the human figure; I also enjoy landscapes, still lifes, and cityscapes. Currently I am working mostly in oil on linen and oil on canvas. I paint and draw from life/*en plein air* where possible. The point is not just the making of pictures, but equally it is a way of seeing. My usual style is a lyrical realism, which tends to juxtapose unexpected elements into a visual narrative. The intention is that the paintings and drawings are more of a "question mark" that will engage the viewer rather than being a "full stop." Therefore, there is some subversion of realism and a focus on contemporary issues in our culture.

I also love to encourage young people in finding their "voice" in art, and I love to learn from other artists through exhibitions and books.

2. **What struggles have you had as a Christian engaged with the arts?**

My struggles mostly relate to realizing my aims as a Christian engaged in visual art. Those aims are:

to practice art in a way that celebrates the creativity of God and brings him praise
to strive for excellence in art that has contemporary relevance
to be salt and light in the marketplace of ideas that is the contemporary art scene
to be a good friend to fellow artists and draw them toward Christ
to serve the marginalized through art

In the past, the chief struggle was simply to find enough time to devote to art-making. Progress in art is only possible with concentrated and regular hard work. While the challenge of finding time was partly a product of the demands of work and family, the deeper reason was an inner voice. That voice indicated that visual art was "just an indulgence." At times, that remains the view of some Christian friends, which is disappointing.

Another struggle is with the inner voice of self-doubt. How can art be my calling if I seem so inadequate in what I produce? At the other end of the spectrum, when good art is made, pride and ego seem ever keen to take the front seat.

Working beside non-Christian artists as I do, I constantly struggle to find natural ways of "speaking without words" the truths of God—how to be eloquent as a Christian in art-making and in conversations. I want to be an authentic voice for God—not corny, Polyanna-like, formulaic, or full of platitudes. This requires loving and listening to my non-Christian friends and taking to heart the issues of contemporary art with all its seeming contradictions and complexity.

3. Describe the ministry you've been able to have through the arts.

Visual art has given me wonderful friendships with fellow Christian and non-Christian artists. One of the great privileges of a studio environment (at a university and at regular local drawing groups where I live) is the "conversation" of art. Invariably, we explore through art the things that most *matter* to us. We formulate and unpack our obsessions with life, creation, and the human condition. As life is sometimes complex and messy, so too the art produced may at times be unsettling and challenging. At other times, though, it may focus on beauty, order, and "inscape." Inevitably, I find myself in conversations with non-Christian artists who will talk freely of what matters to them and of our human condition (whether or not we like that term). It is a time for listening.

One friend is painting portraits (from Amnesty International photos) of people who have disappeared due to civil violence in south Asia. Another friend is painting about the experience of childhood abuse. Another is painting about our society's obsession with outward beauty but inner chaos. Another is painting the simple joy of seagulls. These friends are honest, open, and willing to be vulnerable. This brings an opportunity to befriend them and to paint as a person of hope. To speak of the dignity of being a person in God's image into this context is a great privilege. Currently my main aim is to speak in painting about personhood: our true nature as great (Psalm 8) but fallen (Romans 3). It is not always easy, and there is no place for platitudes. But it is exciting and it matters.

Within our local church, my wife, Jill, and I are involved in a young adults' Bible study group comprised of members who each have a creative interest (from music and poetry to landscape architecture and computing science). This ministry can encourage the integration of God's creative gifts in the individual with their faith and calling. There are other opportunities, such as encouraging high school students who are studying art to prayerfully find creative ways to honor God on paper or on canvas.

4. Concerning other artists you know, what is the single biggest barrier stopping them from coming to Christ?

In my experience, the biggest barrier to faith in Christ for some artists is their "pigeonholing" of the Christian subculture. To know more about Jesus and to follow him would involve identifying with the "church" as they see it. And often they consider Christians to be a pretty exclusive club. That club, to them, is characterized by conservatism, a degree of intellectual naiveté, self-absorption, and moralizing. The church seems more about rule-makers than life-affirmers.

Added to this is a broader Gen-Y and postmodern mind-set that is, frankly, reluctant to take a *fixed position* on anything, let alone the great matters of life. The joy of the ride is much more fun than ever reaching a destination. Everything is to be questioned and challenged, but woe betide anyone who will personally take hold of absolute truth. To be avant-garde in contemporary art often implies the way of relentless skepticism, critique, and rejection. The position of honor is the agent provocateur, the enfant terrible. A word of hope, however, can be found in the counterview that challenges an individualistic avant-garde, which was expressed in the recent Biennale of Sydney (titled "All Our Relations").

The barriers to faith based on a personal encounter with Jesus break my heart. But we go on, prayerfully and always heeding the motto: "Listen, listen, love, love." Ultimately what matters is to be salt and light among non-Christian artists, working with integrity toward excellence and relevance. And, we must always be ready to give account for the hope within, with every opportunity pointing toward Jesus.

CHAPTER 6

ARTISTS AND CHURCH

Many artists have some kind of church background. This seems especially true of musicians, many of whom begin their musical life in the church. I was reminded of this recently when I preached evangelistically at a church and was talking to a professional musician friend, who had come to hear me speak. We were discussing how he enjoyed the service, which led to his telling me that he was strongly involved in a church growing up, and in fact it was there that he learned to play. He spoke fondly about his churchy youth and how significant it was for his musical development. I commented to him that it's interesting that many musicians have church backgrounds, and he added that he knew many such people in Sydney's professional jazz scene.

The trouble is that my friend no longer attends church, nor do most of our mutual friends with church backgrounds.

We must wonder why that is the case. It is difficult to answer that question without doing some formal statistical research, which is beyond my commitment to writing this book ☺. But if I were to posit a hypothesis, I would suggest that the very gift of the church to these musicians became—ironically, tragically—the force that led them away from church life. The church gave them music, and music took them away.

Let me unpack that hypothesis. I don't believe that there's anything intrinsic about music that is incompatible with church life, but there is a lot about a musician's *lifestyle* that can be highly incompatible. From anecdotal evidence gathered over the years through relationships with musicians, there seems to be two key ways in which a musician's lifestyle can lead them away from church.

The first is the more predictable—perhaps stereotypical—of the two. There is often a strong *party* element among musicians. Staying up all night, excessive use of alcohol, experimentation with drugs, and various other unhealthy lifestyle options are common fare for many. These factors can also be incorporated around the music itself, at late-night jam sessions, after-gig parties, and so on. The fact that such things are almost woven into the musical experience itself means that musicians are frequently exposed to them—many of whom may not have been tempted by them had they not been musicians.

Moreover, the party lifestyle can be accompanied by significant peer *and professional* pressure to partake. A drummer friend of mine once told me that he was fired from a prestigious jazz group because he wasn't interested in getting drunk with the band after every rehearsal. It's astonishing that such discrimination can take place over something like that, but it is very much a reality within some circles of professional music.

These factors can make life difficult for young Christian musicians. At several points in their careers, they will have to choose between Christ and partaking in the shady elements of the musician's lifestyle. When a young musician is trying to establish a place in the scene, peer pressure can be a powerful force. Sadly, many musicians choose the lifestyle. And they eventually—inevitably—leave the church.

Such is the predictable path of Christian artists of various kinds, not just musicians. The visual arts are virtually synonymous with a bohemian lifestyle, characterized by drug and alcohol abuse. Theatrical communities are stereotypically rife with sexual promiscuity, and so it goes. Thus, young Christian artists are exposed to ungodly lifestyles—together with pressure to partake—to a greater degree than most of their nonartistic peers.

The second way in which an artist's lifestyle can become incompatible with church life is less sinister—but equally tragic. Sadly, artists can become alienated from mainstream church life through no fault of their own. They are often poorly understood by "normal" church folk. And I'm not referring to the lack of understanding about the arts that professional artists face on a daily basis. That's a given. I am here referring to the lack of understanding about the *lifestyle* of an artist.

I know Christian musicians who have been given a hard time by church friends about taking gigs on Sunday. It seems that their friends think of a gig as a fun, hobby-type activity, a bit like sports for many people. Just as they wouldn't join a soccer competition that plays its games when church is on, so the musician shouldn't take gigs at that time. But that attitude reveals a failure to understand the nature of the musician's life. For the musician, the gig is their paid work. It is the source of their income and puts food on the table. Moreover, most gigs are on weekends; that is the important part of the week for the working musician. Added to those factors is the attitude that many musicians share (rightly or wrongly): if they reject a gig when it's offered, they won't be considered next time.

Putting those factors together, you can see why a musician needs to work on Sundays if the work is offered. It's interesting to compare the attitude of churchgoers on this issue compared to, say, how they might think about a doctor who needs to work a weekend shift at the hospital. A doctor working on the weekend would probably not raise an eyebrow, but the musician who does a gig instead of going to church just doesn't have his priorities sorted out. Is this because medical work is considered to be "important," but music is indulgent? Is it because a doctor may have no control over her hours, but a musician can choose whether or not to do a gig? Whatever the reason, it seems clear to me that such attitudes are fairly typical within churches, and they contribute to artist-alienation.

The Sunday gig is not the only misunderstood element of the musician's lifestyle. How they spend the rest of their week can also raise suspicion among church people. If a musician typically plays late-night gigs, they will be late risers. They may spend much of their day practicing or rehearsing.

They may just relax and recover during the day. To many "normal" Christians, this way of living may appear lazy and self-indulgent. And if they have so much free time, why not use it to serve the church in some way?

I remember once being told that instead of practicing six hours a day, I should use that time for prayer. It was a well-meaning comment, but one that made me feel totally alienated (and guilty every time I practiced instead of praying). The woman who said that to me revealed that she did not consider practice as a legitimate form of "work" that contributes to my career. It was a waste of time—a luxury at best. If I had had the foresight at the time, I would have replied that she ought to quit her job too so we could pray all day together.

Painters and other visual artists suffer similar misunderstandings. I remember attending a Bible study once at an artist's home. His house was a mess, with paint, canvases, and brushes lying all over the place. It had "bohemian" written all over it, as, indeed, did the painter himself, with his cultivated, disheveled appearance! At the beginning of the Bible study, people shared what they had been doing during the week, and most of the "normal" Christians talked about their work in "ordinary" office jobs. My friend the painter talked about how he was struggling to capture the right light on a canvas he was working on. Mixing paint, repainting, artistic frustration—these were the issues that consumed his week.

The "normal" Christians in the group no doubt found this weird. They had worked and contributed to their business, public service, or whatever, but what had the painter contributed? What had he achieved? It was hard to say. They were too polite to intimate any such thing, of course, but it was written on their faces. I decided to chime in with a further anecdote of artistic "struggle" by talking about my saxophone practice that week and the tunes I was trying to master. This whole experience at the painter's house was just another example of the fact that artists are poorly understood by church folk.

The failure of many churches to understand artists leads to their failure to care for artists. Instead of being supported in a difficult and spiritually precarious occupation, artists are judged or neglected. Instead of alienating a musician who cannot regularly attend a Sunday gathering, churches ought to consider how they can edify and equip the Christian musician. How they can prepare the artist to grow as a believer in a spiritually risky career? That may mean providing the musician with some form of fellowship during the week rather than the weekend. In fact, in an effort to minister to Christian artists and evangelize non-Christian artists, my friend Richard Maegraith began a congregation tailor-made for artists—on Monday afternoons! As a participant in that congregation, I could sense that the musicians there felt loved because their Sundays were now freed up for guilt-free paying work.

I'm not suggesting that the only way to care for artists in your church is to start a whole new congregation to cater for their needs and lifestyle. But the thinking of church leaders needs to be creative if they want to minister to creative people. They are different. They are poorly understood. Their lives don't fit the typical mold. If we're serious about their lives in Christ, we must step up in our thinking, strategy, and care. Artists can make a wonderful contribution to the kingdom of Christ. Let's not curtail that potential just because our artists are "fringy" and require a bit of extra thought and effort.

All of this is to say that if churches want to be serious about reaching artistic communities for Christ, they should begin with the artists they already have. We ought to make ministry to such people the first step in reaching the subcultures to which they belong. Let's put a stop to the typical phenomenon of artists being pushed to the fringe of church life. After all, the first step toward growth is the prevention of decline. Make sure we're not *losing* artists before we turn our attention to reaching out to unchurched artists. These are the people God has already given us, so we must fulfill our responsibility before God to make sure they are built up in Christ and become mature in the faith, so that they can live their lives for Christ as artists.

Karl Birchley

Artist Profile: Keith Birchley

1. **Describe your artistic interests.**

My interests are primarily in what is loosely called "classical music," but more specifically in the repertoire of the period of music history technically termed the *Classical Period*—that is, the second half of the eighteenth century, epitomized by the figures of Haydn and Mozart. My favorite composers are Mozart, Chopin, Bach, and Schubert, though I have a deep appreciation of many others. As a pianist, the piano repertoire is high in my affections, but hardly alone. Anything in the high "art music" of the Western tradition does far more than interest me. In thinking of the greatest works of art ever, I have a delightful inward tussle between, on the one hand, the operas and piano concertos of Mozart, and the church cantatas of J. S. Bach on the other. How good of God to give us both!

My second great love aesthetically—though I have never studied it professionally—is literature, especially poetry. After Shakespeare (who is the father of us all!), my dearest writer is the Jesuit poet Gerard Manley Hopkins. His sonnets have been (memorized) friends for many years. Yeats, Eliot, and Les Murray are high in my esteem.

2. What struggles have you had as a Christian engaged with the arts?

My main struggle is how much to engage with them, given the great priority of the work of the gospel. Since conversion to Christ (at the age of twenty), my life has been seesawing back and forth between the equally valid but differently dominant priorities of the doctrines of creation and redemption—how to configure the interface/connection/continuity/discontinuity between the two. My current Master's thesis on the effect of Mozart on Karl Barth grew out of this wider theological complex that has been the backdrop of my theological thinking for thirty years.

An ongoing struggle for me is the dearth of just about any true aesthetic sense in so much of our evangelical, low-church life and public worship. I rarely actually *enjoy* the music at church, and I have had to resolve the issue by not addressing it. The default position for me has been that church is for worship and edification, where I must be only one member of a large body of Christ. Aesthetic sensibilities have to be expressed and realized elsewhere.

Part of this "ache" for me concerns the other side of this aesthetic and creational disinterest. That is the prevalence and dominance of utilitarian and functional categories in so much of the life of evangelicalism. We seem to find it hard to justify (let alone enjoy) something for its own sake, rather than for that to which it is perceived to lead (usually evangelism or Bible teaching). It makes the Christian life barren, joyless, colorless, and task-oriented.

3. Describe the ministry you've been able to have through the arts.

I think largely that my obvious enjoyment of the good things of God preaches its own message. Eleven years ago, while on long-service leave, I put on a series of recitals and produced a CD entitled "Every Good Gift." The title was a conflation of 1 Timothy 6:17 and James 1:17. The purpose was simply the enjoyment of the good gifts of God, whether Mozart's or Haydn's abilities, or my own. It was softly pre-evangelistic, as I introduced the pieces with all sorts of reflections, a few of them theological.

In church and theological circles I have been seeking to preach the "gospel" of creation for some years now, concerned that in our desire to affirm the primacy of reconciliation/redemption we become unfortunately guilty of a negation of creation, which is neither honoring to God nor helpful for ourselves.

4. **Concerning other artists you know, what is the single biggest barrier stopping them from coming to Christ?**

   To be honest, it would be idolatry—the idolatry of worshiping and serving the art form rather than the Supreme Artist. Artists and highly expressive people tend to be by definition self-conscious and self-absorbed. If they weren't this way, they wouldn't command our attention and bless our lives. But such a temperament is difficult to mix amicably with the devotions and disciplines of the Christian life.

CHAPTER 7

DETHRONING THE IDOL

The central issue in outreach to artists is idolatry. Yes, the chief problem facing the evangelism of artists is that their god is art. Of course idolatry is not unique to artistic communities and is no doubt equally serious for outreach to all kinds of people. Money can be god; success can be god; popularity, relationships, pleasure, sports, power, and self can all be god, and frequently are for most unbelievers.

But for artists, this goes deep. Take a professional musician. These people did not just choose to study music at university and decide to become a musician, as though music was like engineering or commerce. No, to study music at an elite level, they must have been devoted to music for most of their lives to that point. I began learning piano at the age of six, saxophone at twelve. By the time I was finishing high school, I had already practiced either piano or saxophone for literally thousands of hours. And this was before even becoming "professional."

On top of the thousands of hours of dedication, artists develop their identity around their art form. I remember a conversation I had with one of my uncle's colleagues when I was seventeen. I was still a high school student at the time, and my uncle's colleague asked me what I did for work. I said I was a musician. My uncle later pointed out to me that he found it interesting that I would say I was a musician rather than say that I was still at school. I just didn't identify myself as a school student; I was a musician.

For many serious artists, art becomes the most important thing in life before they've finished school. They have already selected their career and are already working toward it. Their priorities are shaped around art, practicing, their future careers, and "making it." In my final two years of high school, I basically ignored all my other studies. I practiced saxophone four hours a day—during the school day and at night. While my fellow school students were hitting the books to get into the university courses they wanted, I played saxophone. Scales, tunes, long notes, reeds, listening, transcribing, and gigs were my life. Nothing else mattered. I think that would be pretty typical of many professional artists. The idolatry starts early and goes deep.

Once an artist reaches university-level study (if, indeed, they bother with that), their idolatry is confirmed and encouraged. No one at music school ever told me directly to make music my god, but the message was clear. In a thousand different ways, we were taught that if we wanted any chance to make it as a professional musician, music would need to be the most important thing in life. It's okay to have a girlfriend, but don't let that get in the way. Family? Okay, but again, keep your priorities straight. You need to work, work, work, and then work some more. Live and breathe music. It's got to be everything, or you might as well drop out now. You're not going to make it without total devotion. It's that simple.

We had plenty of illustrations of this. One of my lecturers had lived in New York for ten years—the mecca of the jazz world. In order to live there as an Australian, he got married to an American woman so he could get a green card. Yes, that's right. Music was more important than marriage; the latter was simply a ticket for the former in this guy's life. When it was time for him to move back to Australia, he simply got a divorce. Those artists who had not gone to such extremes for their art, were, predictably, less successful and less respected. By the time an artist leaves university-level study of their art, they will either have decided not to pursue the idol—because they will have decided they do not have the commitment to make it, or perhaps they lacked the talent—or they will be fully-fledged priests in the idolatry of art.

The idolatry is not just about "making it" or identity; it's more complex than that. Most artists have a deep passion and love for what they do. Their years of devotion and service to the god comes with a deeply felt love and affection. It may be their love that drove them to dedication, or sometimes the love comes as a result of their dedication. Either way, it's a deeply personal and cherished part of their lives. This means that even artists who have no desire to "make it" in terms of their career (or have given up trying to do so) might nevertheless treat art as an idol. In fact, to one way of thinking, that is an even purer form of idolatry, since the trappings of fame and fortune are not relevant; it's only about the art, man! Not only is this so, but for many, their art "saves" them somehow. It gives life meaning and purpose. It makes them matter. It gives them status and a place within a community.

If we have any hope at all of reaching an artist for Christ, the major challenge will be to dethrone the idol. In the end, the artist must choose whether they will worship art or Christ. Everything else depends on this. But before we explore how this might be achieved, it's important to understand the place of art in God's good creation.

Wonderful Servant, Terrible Master

While art might become an idol, it is not in and of itself bad or sinful. Of course not! It's a wonderful part of God's creation, designed for our enjoyment, nourishment, psychological well-being, expression, and personhood. It is undeniably a wonderful gift from God. It's very important to come to grips with a theological understanding of art before challenging the idol of art. There are a couple of good reasons for this. First, because we should know the truth, regardless. God created the arts. They are good. Second, we must realize that the goal of dethroning the idol of art is not to vanquish art. Just because it has become an idol does not mean that it must be destroyed.

Unfortunately, too many Christians react inappropriately to the thing that has become an idol, whether that be art, sports, money, or whatever. But it's not that the *thing* is wrong—it's that someone's attitude and treatment of the thing is wrong. Just because money is the idol of many people does not make money an evil thing in itself. In fact, the Bible teaches that wealth is a gift from God. Just because sex is an idol for others does not make sex evil. It is also the gift of God. It's our attitude toward it and our treatment of it that's the issue. So it is with the arts. Some people have made art into an idol. The idol must be dethroned, but the main issue is about one's attitude toward art, not art itself.

Having said that, art is a wonderful servant but a terrible master. This is the case for all forms of idolatry. The gift of God—wonderful as it is—can become a terrible curse if abused. This is true for money, sex, sports, relationships, and, well, just about everything God has given us. They are great gifts, but if abused, they can do great damage. Just consider how damaging sex can be when not engaged according to God's design, within the covenant of marriage between a man and woman. The total devastation that money and power can create when abused can destroy entire nations.

Make no mistake: the idolatry of art can do great damage to people's lives. It can destroy relationships, families, mental and physical health, and virtually everything good in life. That's what idols do: they destroy. They might appear attractive for worship, but they are not good gods. Only Christ is worthy of worship, and only he can fix broken lives. When he is magnified, everything else is put in its right place. And this includes art. Art has its place. For Christian artists, it will occupy an important place, but this cannot be first place.

And that's the key to helping Christian artists and to reaching non-Christian ones. We need to affirm the wonder and beauty of art, but also teach that it is not god. We have no business telling an artist that they must quit their art if they want to be a Christian. No, their gift is from Christ; who are we to take that away? The secret is not to pit art and Christ against one another in such a way that only one will be left standing. They are in competition only if art is occupying Christ's position as number one. Once he is recognized as Lord, art will find its place. Its place is under him. As the creator of art and giver of all gifts, Christ is not necessarily interested in vanquishing art; he is only concerned to dethrone it as idol.

Giving It Up?

Some artists, however, may feel that they need to give up their art—at least for a time—in order to make Christ Lord of their lives. I know two guys who fall in this category. One is a supremely gifted guitarist in Canberra; we all used to be in awe of his natural ability, unmatched technique, and just sheer genius. I was positive that he was set to become the best jazz guitarist in Australia. But when he became a Christian, he felt he needed to stop playing guitar. I thought this was terribly sad, and I tried to talk him out of it, but he had his reasons. For him, guitar had become such a powerful idol that he simply could not play without it conflicting with his love for Christ. Not only that, but his history of drug and alcohol abuse were both tied to music; he couldn't escape those demons without putting the guitar down. You have to respect that, as sad as it is. He realized that to dethrone the idol of his heart, it needed to be completely rooted out.

My other friend is a drummer. When he became a Christian, he felt similarly about the power of the idol in his life.

He stopped playing drums. But in this friend's case, he took up playing guitar and became quite good at that instead. The change of instrument enabled a break with the old idol, but it also allowed his love of music to continue, and he used it particularly in gospel and church settings in New York. Now I am pleased to say that he is playing the drums again, has recorded his first album, and is doing gigs in New York—and all with Christ as Lord! Praise God!

My own story is a little different again. I didn't ever stop playing saxophone, but the battle between Jazz and Jesus in my life wasn't finally over until I was willing to give it all up. In my final year of studying jazz performance at university I decided to pursue full-time vocational ministry once my studies were complete, having become a Christian in my first year. It was a really tough decision, and I was sure it would mean that I would stop playing. It was effectively a decision to quit playing jazz because I thought that once I stop practicing four hours a day, I wouldn't be able to play anymore. So, when the new year came around, I began working full-time as a ministry apprentice at Crossroads Christian Church in Canberra—where I had become a Christian—and stopped practicing saxophone.

The funny thing is, people still kept booking me to do gigs. I kept doing gigs and discovered that I could still play, even though I had stopped practicing. In fact, I even kept improving! As long as the gigs were there, I could still play. And I was overjoyed! I really felt that I had given up music for Christ, and Christ gave it right back to me. I still play to this day, and I think I can honestly say that I am now a better musician than I have ever been.

But the point of my story is that something radical happened in that first year of "giving up music." The decision to give it up meant that the idol was finally destroyed. Christ was Lord of my life, and now without any competition. Music remained a part of my life, but it had been put in its proper place. And Christ gave music back to me in more ways than one. Not only could I continue to play, but I fell in love with music all over again.

You see, one of the unfortunate consequences of taking music too seriously is that it can cease to be that innocent, playful, and fun activity that drew me to it in the first place. That playful and fun element returned to music for me once I "quit." I realized that this is how it was always meant to be: music is for *enjoyment* and pleasure; if you take it too seriously, it can cease to be what it is meant to be. Ever since that time, playing jazz has been a sheer joy for me precisely because it doesn't matter too much. I'm not trying to impress everyone so I can get gigs and make a living or career out of it. I just play for fun. And I thank God for its role in my life.

The lessons I've learned from my own experience have helped me in outreach to other musicians. I talk to them about the role of music in life and God's intention for it. I affirm its goodness and wonder. I affirm the things they love about it. But then I turn to say that I think music has become god in their life. I try to show them how it has shaped who they are, what's most important to them, and the big decisions in life. Then I try to argue that, while music is great, it's not god. And in fact, it is probably making their life miserable. I ask them if they can remember back to their first love of music—how much fun it was, and the sheer joy of creating and listening.

The professional musicians I talk to often resonate with this; they kind of miss music, even though they play it all the time. It has become a job. A career. A thing that must be developed in order to make money. And their idolatry of music has killed their love of it. They serve it because they have to. It rules them, but their joy has dried up. When my friends acknowledge this much, I feel like I'm getting somewhere. I say to them that I think music ought to be *about* life. But it's not meant to *be* life. The problem with so many musicians is that music has become their life, and so it can no longer be *about* life. How can music be used to express life in this world if it *is* life in this world?

If there is any hope for an artist to be converted to Christ, he or she must first appreciate that their art form has most likely taken the place that only Christ deserves. It has become an idol that must be dethroned. However, a decision for Christ need not be an either/or; that is, choose Christ and give up art. No, it can be a both/and thing. Choose Christ and put art in its proper place. There most certainly is a place for it in the Christian life—a lovely and significant place. But its place is not at the top. Only Christ can live there.

Modeling the Alternative

Nothing helps an artist to learn and understand better than a good model. Artists are wired to learn through imitation. They develop their own style and "voice," as it were, but this nearly always comes about through the close study and imitation of others. If, by the grace of God, an artist comes to Christ, he or she will need to learn what it looks like to have Christ in first place while also being committed to art.

It won't be enough simply to say, "Now, go live with Christ as Lord, and with art no longer as god." How that is meant to work out in one's life as an artist is far from clear.

As such, the ideal scenario is for a newborn Christian artist to be discipled by a mature Christian artist. They could hang out, talk about the issues facing them both as Christian artists, share each other's lives, and spur one another on to love and good deeds. No one will get what the new Christian artist is going through better than someone who has gone through it too. A mature Christian artist who has the vision and love to get alongside a new convert in this way could do immeasurable good.

This might be the ideal scenario, but for many churches no such mature Christian artist exists. In that case, the newborn Christian artist will still need the Christian life modeled to him or her, even if that is not precisely wired along the lines of professional artistry. The two key things to be modeled, I think, are not surprising. What it looks like for Christ to be Lord needs to be modeled—as does how to appreciate God's good gifts while not committing idolatry.

Sure, it would help to be a lover of the arts and artists. For me, I was blessed to have people around me who did both things. They weren't into jazz, but they loved music. They weren't professional artists, but they were highly capable people who could have done well at anything. But they modeled what it looked like for Christ to be Lord. He was number one, and this was clear through a myriad of small and great actions, words, thoughts, and attitudes. It permeated everything; there was no part of their lives that was not subject to Christ. Or, if there was, there was a live struggle to "put it down."

Through their model and example, I gradually understood how living with Christ as Lord would affect my attitude about music. It was not exceptional; there was no special license to retain just this one thing as an idol. Nope. It had to be put down. But then these friends of mine also modeled what it was like to love and enjoy good things that God has made. Their love of music, coffee, football, Formula One, and so on, taught me that it was okay to embrace the good. Just because these things could potentially become idols did not mean that they were to be shunned. No, they belong to God's good creation and are for our good, to the praise of his glory!

I suppose any pastor knows the importance of discipleship and modeling the Christian life to new believers. I'm simply saying that in that process, it is worth keeping in mind the significance of these twin concerns: the lordship of Christ and the proper embrace of art. How those two things go together will be the key to the Christian artist's maturity and growth. Rather than cause the artist to think poorly of the gifts God has given them, churches ought to encourage godly engagement with the arts—in service of God, and just because it is good.

David Elsey

Artist Profile: Hayley Neal

1. **Describe your artistic interests.**
   I have been involved in the visual performing arts, theater acting, and arts and cultural management.

2. **What struggles have you had as a Christian engaged with the arts?**
   I pursued acting straight out of high school and began a Creative Arts degree at Macquarie University with the view to end up auditioning for the National Institute of Dramatic Art (NIDA) soon after that degree was finished.

   In the last year of my university degree, I encountered Jesus, and life's priorities began to shift and change. Before becoming a Christian, pursuing artistic interests was very much about me: my expression, my enjoyment, my success. Once I became a Christian I really began to see how my pursuits were selfish and not God-honoring. Because of the nature of my art being so tied up with the marketing, promotion, training, and applause of the self, I struggled to see how a Christian could actually be an actor. It seemed to be an occupation that fostered pride and enabled a hedonistic lifestyle to flourish.

I tried to invest my creativity into Creative Arts ministries but soon became frustrated. In my Christian circles there seemed to be an emphasis on the proclamation of the gospel, and everything else—if it didn't aid that—was a waste of time. I weighed up the amount of time to create something compared to the time it took to create a Bible talk or Scripture lesson and asked myself: What is a better use of my time?

These questions are not specific only to being an artist or being creative, but they relate also to the fact that I did have gifts for teaching and evangelism and so wanted to make the most of life for Christ with the gifts I had and be most effective for the kingdom.

A talk from John Piper has helped immensely in weighing up the dichotomy that seems to exist; you can listen to Piper's talk at www.desiringgod.org/resource-library/ask-pastor-john/what-is-the-value-of-art-in-the-church.

3. Describe the ministry you've been able to have through the arts.

I have led the creation of certain cultural events: *I Heart Kirribilli Art Exhibition and Prize* as well as *Carols under the Bridge*.

I Heart Kirribilli is a multifaceted event that celebrates community and encourages and supports artists, while propelling the church to do evangelism by living missionally among the residents and artists of Kirribilli, Sydney.

I Heart creates places for smiling faces. A space where locals, churchgoers, and nonchurchgoers alike can hang out. We design the event so that there is a reason for guests, who come to view the exhibition, to engage with one another as well as to engage with the Christian community at our church.

I Heart seeks to support artists. Our church absorbs the financial costs of this event. We dedicate $3,500 to prize money. Past winners have commented on how the generosity of the church with these prizes astounds them. Not only that church would see the arts as a worthwhile thing, but that, as an artist whose average wage is about $10,000 to $15,000 annually, $1,000 – and the recognition of winning a prize – is valuable to their soul and pocket. One winner commented that the air-conditioning in his (and his heavily pregnant wife's) car had busted the week of *I Heart* – the cost: $750. The prize money he won? $750. He wrote us a card saying,

"Someone must be looking out for us." Also, giving artists a platform for their work to be viewed and celebrated helps to encourage their creativity.

I Heart is missional. We seek to use the exhibition and prizes as a way to bless our community but also to bring them up close to our church community. As the thousands of people walk through the transformed space of our church building, our church family greets them, engages in conversation, and seeks to befriend someone new during the week of *I Heart* for the sake of the gospel. The prize night has an explicit gospel talk from the judges as they articulate an apologetic related to the zeitgeist/curatorial theme. The prize night is filled with the artists who have entered the competition (80 percent of whom are unchurched), with their families and friends. Hundreds of people who normally have very little contact with Christianity enjoy a great night and positive interaction with both the church and the gospel.

I am also one of the cofounders of the Sydney Artists' Retreat. Helen, Jess, and I created this annual long weekend in 2012 after seeing a great need to encourage and connect to Christian artists. We believe that the health of your faith informs the health of your art. Therefore, we try to ensure that the retreat gives space for artists to reflect, pray, worship, and meditate on God's Word, enjoy fellowship, collaborate with other artists, and dedicate time to their own art practice—whether that be singing, painting, jewelry making, dance, poetry, or multimedia.

4. **Concerning other artists you know, what is the single biggest barrier stopping them from coming to Christ?**
   Christianity is too straight. There is only one path. It is a narrow means of knowing something. Christianity doesn't seem to promote individuality, freedom, or creative expression. It appears more as a strait-jacket or a crutch. Some friends have said to me, "You go to church; we go to shrinks."

CONCLUSION

God is the ultimate Artist. He is the Creator of all things. He delights in color, sound, shapes of all kinds, and unstraight lines. Every person he has made is entirely unique. What an artist is he! Not only does God create, but he re-creates too. In Christ Jesus, we who were bent out of shape, distorted, and rebellious creatures are transformed into the likeness of Christ. God's life-giving Spirit indwells us, recasting our inclinations and the desires of our hearts that we might love and honor our Creator. We are the very artistry of God! We are the products of his handiwork and the pinnacle of his creation. God delights in his creation, his re-creation, his people. It is little wonder that the Creator God should see fit to bring the arts into the service of his work of re-creation. What could be more appropriate? The creative arts involved in the re-creation of people.

It is a privilege to be a servant of the gospel. It is a privilege to be an artist. It is a special privilege to serve the gospel through the arts. As I reflect on the various ways in which God has employed the arts as a vehicle for the gospel in my experience, I pray for all artists around the world. For

Christian artists, I pray they will continue to give thanks for the gifts God has given them and for the privilege of being creators, as he is. I also pray that they will know the joy of being artistic ambassadors of Jesus Christ. May they appreciate the symbiosis of creation and re-creation. May they not regard "using" the arts for outreach a kind of crass utilitarianism, but see that creativity and re-creativity belong together in the mind of God.

For artists who do not yet know God, I pray that the very process of creation will cause them to give thought to the Creator. I pray that their artistic communities will not be devoid of Christ, but that artists will meet, respect, and bond with believers. May such believers speak a powerful word into those artistic communities. A word of creation and re-creation, a word about the purpose of life, a word of faith, hope, and love.

And I pray for the churches. May they embrace the arts as God's good gift. May they encourage, equip, and inspire the artists in their midst. May they understand the challenges and peculiarities that artists face, offering a safe haven of respect and love rather than misunderstanding and judgment. May the churches form partnerships with believing artists for the sake of the gospel. May the partnership of creativity and re-creativity become a powerful alliance in churches everywhere.

And I pray that churches will have a heart for all unreached people groups. May they reach out to the artistic communities around them. May they show love and acceptance to unbelieving artists, who will, through them, catch a glimpse of the awesome love of God in Christ.

Keep Your Greek

Strategies for Busy People

Constantine R. Campbell

Some ministry leaders have to spend countless hours mastering biblical languages while they are in seminary. They must learn how the knowledge of these languages illuminates the reading, understanding, and application of Scripture. But while excellent language acquisition resources abound, few really teach these leaders how to maintain their use of Greek for the long term. Consequently, pastors and other former Greek students find that under the pressures of work, ministry, preaching, and life, their hard-earned Greek skills begin to disappear.

Con Campbell has been counseling one-time Greek students for years, teaching them how to keep their language facility for the benefit of those to whom they minister and teach. He shows how following the right principles makes it possible for many to retain—and in some cases regain—their Greek language skills.

Ministry leaders will find *Keep Your Greek* an encouraging and practical guide to strengthening their Greek abilities so that they can make linguistic insights a regular part of their study and teaching. Current students will learn how to build skills that will serve them well once they complete their formal language instruction.

Available in stores and online!

Share Your Thoughts

With the Author: Your comments will be forwarded to the author when you send them to *zauthor@zondervan.com.*

With Zondervan: Submit your review of this book by writing to *zreview@zondervan.com.*

Free Online Resources at www.zondervan.com

Zondervan AuthorTracker: Be notified whenever your favorite authors publish new books, go on tour, or post an update about what's happening in their lives at www.zondervan.com/authortracker.

Daily Bible Verses and Devotions: Enrich your life with daily Bible verses or devotions that help you start every morning focused on God. Visit www.zondervan.com/newsletters.

Free Email Publications: Sign up for newsletters on Christian living, academic resources, church ministry, fiction, children's resources, and more. Visit www.zondervan.com/newsletters.

Zondervan Bible Search: Find and compare Bible passages in a variety of translations at www.zondervanbiblesearch.com.

Other Benefits: Register to receive online benefits like coupons and special offers, or to participate in research.